George Goldsmith-Carter

Sailing Ships
& Sailing Craft

illustrated by Bill Robertshaw

Hamlyn · London
Sun Books · Melbourne

FOREWORD

The two primary causes which led to the evolution of sailing transport were the urges to migrate and to trade. Both led in turn to conflict, so there evolved three basic types of vessels: vessels to carry migrants, to carry goods, and for fighting.

The development of particular types of sailing vessels, as with other forms of evolution, was irregular. In some instances the process was a slow but steady forward movement through the centuries. Ideas were exchanged gradually and new designs adopted, often from widely differing sources. An outstanding example is provided by the sailing vessels of the eleventh and fourteenth centuries, in which the stability of the 'round ship' of the early Mediterranean peoples is combined with the seaworthiness and speed of the Norse longships.

This process of development continued into the nineteenth century, culminating perhaps in the clipper ships, which have been described as 'mankind's most beautiful creation'. On the other hand, while some ship-forms underwent endless metamorphosis, other forms remained static: the Irish curragh has hardly changed in a thousand years, for example, while the galley has entirely disappeared.

We are grateful to the many Institutions and individuals who have helped to make this book so authoritative. They are fully listed on page 156.

The author adds his own appreciation for the unstinted help given by Captain A. V. Harris of Deal (a member of that exclusive brotherhood, 'The Cape Horners' Club').

Published by The Hamlyn Publishing Group Limited
London · New York · Sydney · Toronto
Hamlyn House, Feltham, Middlesex, England
In association with Sun Books Pty, Melbourne

ISBN 0 600 00116 4

Phototypeset by Oliver Burridge Filmsetting Limited, Crawley, Sussex
Colour separations by Schwitter Limited, Zurich
Printed in England by Sir Joseph Causton & Sons Limited

CONTENTS

SAILING VESSELS OF THE ANCIENT WORLD

Egypt

Egyptians seem to have been the first to build ships. In 1929, Sir Flinders Petrie unearthed a stone model of a sailing craft estimated to be 11,000 years old at Fayim. These vessels were essentially river craft, used only for sailing with the wind. Although they hated the sea, the Egyptians did build sea-going vessels, for around 2900 BC Pharaoh Sneferu assembled forty wooden ships and sent them to Byblos in Phoenicia to trade for cedar wood. They were without keels or frames, being built of short blocks of *acacia nilotica*, or sunt, pegged together like bricks. The bipod mast was counterbalanced with stones, so that it could be lowered to the deck when the vessel was under oars. Steering was by six oars, whilst the purely non-functional stem- and stern-posts were ornamented with the Eye of Horus and the Sacred Ankh, or Symbol of Life.

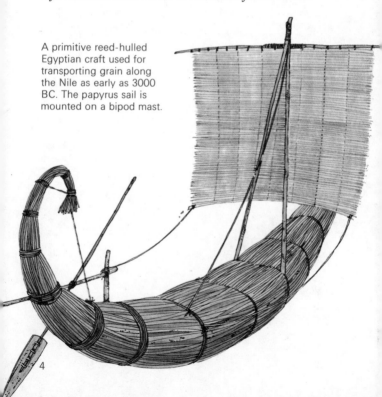

A primitive reed-hulled Egyptian craft used for transporting grain along the Nile as early as 3000 BC. The papyrus sail is mounted on a bipod mast.

4

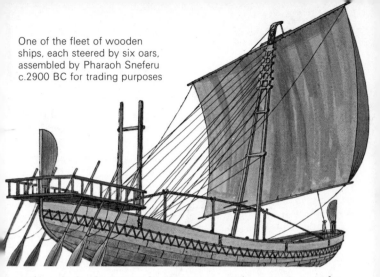

One of the fleet of wooden
ships, each steered by six oars,
assembled by Pharaoh Sneferu
c.2900 BC for trading purposes

Bas reliefs of 1200 BC depict Rameses III's victory over the
Philistines in the first-known naval battle. They show warships
with metal-shod rams. One powerful steering oar had now
replaced the six individually manned oars described above. A
single mast, conventionally stayed, carried the first ever
'fighting top'. The large, well-designed sails were brailed so
that they could be furled without being lowered. High-planked
bulwarks protected the rowers. These ships marked the zenith
of shipbuilding in Ancient Egypt. Indeed, some Nile craft today
are cruder than their ancient prototypes.

Warship of Rameses III,
with battering-ram

Nile gaiassa

Boatbuilders on the Nile still lack suitable timber. Sunt and sycamore grow only in short lengths, and although hard are brittle and difficult to work. Craft are made of planks four to six feet long which are joined to form longer planks, which gives the vessels an inherent weakness; built by 'rule of thumb', they are rough and ungainly.

The two- and three-masted, lateen-rigged gaiassa, like a Thames sailing barge, is a maid of all work. Unlike Thames barges, however, gaiassas do not sail against the wind, only with it, and then drift back with the current.

The Dongola markab, found on the Dongola Reach of the Nile, is like the gaiassa, but with one well-stayed mast amidships. The sail is slung obliquely from the masthead and has two yards, one at the head and one at the foot of the sail. It is a shallow-draught all-purpose vessel, with a powerful rudder.

The nuggar, found in the vicinity of Omdurman, is a crudely built, shallow-draught vessel, undecked, broad in the beam and carrying a single mast stepped amidships. It is propelled by a sail almost identical to that of the markab. The nuggar is most frequently used as a ferry boat, and smaller nuggars may serve as tenders to the larger ones. The largest type of nuggar is approximately sixty-two feet overall, has a crew of six to eight men, and carries cargoes of between forty and fifty tons.

Dongola markab

Nile nuggar

Early Arab sailing vessels

Early nomadic Arabs hated and feared the sea even more than the Ancient Egyptians, for the Prophet Mohammed preached to his followers: 'He who twice embarks upon the sea is truly an infidel.'

Nevertheless, the Arabs, and particularly the Saracens, were a virile and fearless people who, after encountering the mariners of Phoenicia and Greece, quickly grasped the significance of naval power and sea trade.

Thus they soon learned not only how to design and build

The two-masted, lateen-rigged baghla, an Arab ship of striking appearance

The fast, shallow-draught zaruk

ships, but how to navigate them with skill and use them with ferocity in war. In AD 649 a great Saracen fleet captured the island of Cyprus and a few years later defeated the Greek fleet off the coast of Lycia.

Today the Arabs have their own distinctive types of sailing vessels known collectively by Europeans, but not by the Arabs, as dhows.

Most impressive of all the Arabs' sailing ships is the shapely and seaworthy baghla, a two-masted, lateen-rigged vessel which incorporates many innovations of both hemispheres. The lofty, ornately carved and decorated poop is similar to that of a fifteenth-century caravel (see page 74), whilst the massive rudder is housed in a rudder trunk after the manner of the old East Indiamen. Also reminiscent of the caravel is the carvel-built hull of the baghla, on which the planks are laid edge-to-edge instead of overlapping.

The sleekly sinister zaruk, a fast, shallow-draught, single-masted, lateen-rigged vessel used for the coastal trade in the Gulf of Aden, the Persian Gulf and the Red Sea, is of unusual design which, unlike that of the baghla, shows no European

The sambuk, a two-masted, lateen-rigged vessel from the Red Sea

influence. The bow rakes sharply forward and the narrow rudder extends well below the keel and is operated by an unusual arrangement of blocks and tackles. Because of its speed, handiness and the shallow draught which permitted it to elude capture by slipping across shoals and sandbanks, the zaruk was favoured even up to comparatively recent times by slavers, gun-runners and smugglers, especially ivory smugglers. Also used by pearl-diving communities, the zaruk is sometimes known as the garookuh.

The graceful, carvel-built, two-masted, lateen-rigged sambuk of the Red Sea, like the baghla, shows definite early-

European influence in its forward-raking masts and built-up poop deck, the quarters of which are decorated with gaily painted lozenges, arcades and bands, after the manner of an Elizabethan galleon.

The single-masted, lateen-rigged badan, most frequently seen in the waters around Aden, like the zaruk, was frequently used for all manner of nefarious schemes because of its speed, ease of handling and shallow draught. This vessel has the same distinctive rudder and steering gear as the zaruk whilst the stem-piece is almost straight, lacking the extreme rake which is characteristic of the zaruk.

Both zaruk and badan, unlike the larger, square-sterned baghla, have sharp sterns, a feature which makes both types of vessel particularly suitable for handling in heavy following seas or heavy surf.

The badan, most commonly found near Aden, a coastal ship favoured by smugglers grateful for her speed and ease of handling

Ivory model of a
boat found at
Knossos

Ancient Crete

So far as can be established, the first people ever to build *seagoing* sailing vessels were the Neolithic inhabitants of Crete, who are known to have exported obsidian, a volcanic flint suitable for the manufacture of edged implements and weapons, to Egypt, as long ago as 3000 BC. They also imported material from the Lipari Isles, near Sicily.

With the discovery of tin and copper and the advent of the Bronze Age, shipbuilding in the Mediterranean and the Near East received a tremendous stimulus, for the demand for these metals and for skilled metal-workers created the additional demand for capacious and seaworthy ships to carry them, as well as the metalware, pottery, skins, sponges, wine, olive oil and dried fish that Crete also exported. Thus the early Cretans built large fleets of trading vessels, loaded them with rich cargoes and sailed to every port in the Mediterranean, to the ports of Sicily, to Troy and to Egypt.

Cretan ships with Cretan mariners now dominated sea commerce in the Mediterranean, the Adriatic and the Near East.

Cretan ship engraved on a gold ring discovered at Mochlos

Artist's impression of early Cretan trading vessels

In 1908 an American archaeologist, Professor Seager, whilst excavating on the small, barren island of Mochlos, off Crete, unearthed a unique and splendid hoard of treasure, 4,500 years old. With the hoard was a massive gold ring which shows an engraving of a ship sailing from the shrine of Rhea, the Cretan mother-goddess who was also the protectress of sailors.

Sir Arthur Evans, while excavating the Great Palace of Knossos in Crete at the end of the nineteenth century, unearthed an ivory model of a sailing ship equipped with hold and hatch cover. He also discovered unique maritime seal stones; one such artifact of the Late Minoan Period (1700–1500 BC) was found during the excavation of the ruins of the royal villa near Knossos. It shows a single-masted ship carrying a horse, and was considered by Sir Arthur Evans to record one of the first thoroughbred horses ever imported into Crete. Minoans probably sailed ships of the type depicted on these seal stones to establish their colony on the coast of Palestine about 1200 BC.

Another steatite seal stone of the Early Minoan Period (2800–2200 BC) depicts a ship with two sails and with two crescent moons above the mast (perhaps to show that the voyage lasted two months). Other seals show vessels with one, two and even three masts; one found at Mirabello bears an engraving of a single-masted ship carrying a square sail and equipped with rigging of plaited rawhide ropes of a pattern carried by American clippers of the nineteenth century. Further ship finds in Crete included terracotta and alabaster models found by Italian archaeologists at Aghia Triadha near Phaestos in the vicinity of the Bay of Messara in southern Crete.

The Phoenicians

The Phoenicians left their racial cradle on the north coast of the Persian Gulf in approximately 200 BC to settle in Tyre and Sidon on the east coast of the Mediterranean. From here they sailed to colonize Cadiz, Carthage and Marseilles and the islands of Corsica and Sardinia, and started to compete with Cretan traders.

The Phoenicians, or Sidonians as they called themselves, built stout, seagoing sailing vessels of up to 300 tons' displacement. These had many of the features of both Cretan and Egyptian ships, were single-masted and could only sail with the wind, relying at other times on slave oarsmen. The stem-posts were carved to resemble horses' heads and the inward-curving stern-posts took the form of fish-tails. Piracy was rife: thus Phoenician trading ships were always heavily armed. The Phoenician warship was the bireme, a galley propelled by two banks of oarsmen and carrying a square sail on a mast

Phoenician trading ship.

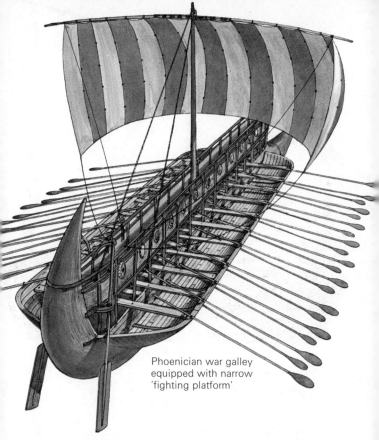

Phoenician war galley
equipped with narrow
'fighting platform'

stepped amidships. The most outstanding characteristic of this
shallow-draught, fast, manoeuvrable, but unseaworthy vessel
was the narrow fighting platform not unlike the 'cat-walk' of a
modern oil tanker. It also had a massive, horn-shaped ram.

The Phoenicians, who have been called the pioneers of the
trade routes, sailed as far north as Britain for Cornish tin. But
they were not true ocean venturers like the later Norsemen,
preferring instead to hug the coast. It seems possible that they
half believed their own horrific tales of sea monsters and
supernatural beings, which they told to other seafarers in order
to keep the secrets of the trade routes to themselves.

Early Greek cargo vessel

Ancient Greece and Rome

The Ancient Greeks became sea-minded about 800 BC. Like the Phoenicians, they founded overseas colonies. Much is known about their war galleys, but little about their trading vessels.

By the second century AD Mediterranean ship design had advanced considerably. Lucian, the Greek satirist, describes the *Isis*, a Roman grain ship he saw in Piraeus, Athens, in AD 150. This vessel was impressive: it was a fully-decked ship with four big holds; its stern post formed the head of a sacred Roman goose, and the bow bore the figurehead of the goddess Isis. Compare her dimensions with those of America's famous Cape Horn clipper *Great Republic*:

Isis: length 180ft; beam 45–50ft; holds 44ft deep.
Great Republic: length 325ft; beam 53ft; holds 38ft deep.

The disparity between the lengths and breadths of these ships shows the difference between the basic Mediterranean 'round-ship' form and the 'longship' form of the Northern sea peoples. Although characteristically Mediterranean, the 'round-ship' had a far-reaching influence on all future ships. The artemon (square bow sail) and awning-covered stern heralded the spritsail and ornate quarter-galleries of European galleons. The bow gallery was to become the fore-castle of medieval ships, and the triangular topsails became the graceful 'moon-rakers' and 'kites' which crowned the Clipper ships.

The *Isis*, a broad-beamed Roman grain-carrier of the 2nd century AD

TRADITIONAL CRAFT

Later Mediterranean vessels

From the third century AD onwards the history of shipbuilding in the Mediterranean is lost, but between the ninth and tenth centuries a revolutionary type of vessel appeared. Its hull was somewhat similar to the Cretan and Greek trading vessels: it was carvel-built (see pages 8–9), the bow raked forward and the stem-post curved inwards. However, the vessel carried two steering oars, and the well-stayed mast, stepped slightly forward of amidships and raked forward at an angle, had a

An early lateen-rigged ship, widely adopted in the 9th and 10th centuries AD by Mediterranean shipbuilders

The Greek dromon, a heavily armoured warship of the 12th century

peculiar hook-shaped masthead and carried a new type of sail, the 'lateen' (a European corruption of the word 'Latin').

The lateen – perhaps of Arab origin – was a right-angled triangular sail laced to a long, sloping yard and controlled by a system of blocks and tackles which enabled the ship to sail against the wind. For the first time in history, sailing vessels which did not need oars appeared in the Mediterranean.

Nevertheless, the many-oared galley with its auxiliary sails was still generally used as a warship, although these too were beginning to change. By the beginning of the twelfth century the cumbersome trireme, with its three banks of oars and a ram, gave way to the formidable dromon (Greek *dromos* = runner).

The dromon carried up to three masts with lateen sails, and although equipped with two banks of oars, handled by 150–200 men, it also bore impressive heavy armament – *ballistae*, giant mechanically operated crossbows which threw javelins, and *catapultae*, which hurled stone balls. Projecting from the bow was a bronze, bellows-operated Greek Fire projector. The armourer was called the *hataphaltaphetes*. Such were the warships used by the Saracens during the Crusades.

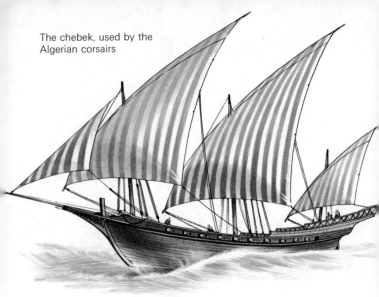

The chebek, used by the
Algerian corsairs

A much later development of the dromon was the chebek, a
swift, shallow-draught vessel used by the Algerian corsairs of
the seventeenth century. The yacht-like chebeks with their
ornately gilded and painted stern and grating deck, carried
heavy cannon and were feared for their formidable performance in battle and their ferocious crews. By 1750 European
influence had changed the chebek to the polacca-chebek.
Although efficient sail design was fast rendering oars obsolete,
galleys were used in battle after 1700. Their slow decline

The polacca-
chebek. Developed
c. 1750 from the
chebek, it carried
an impressive and
highly efficient
combination of
lateen- and square-
rigged sails.

was due to their effectiveness against becalmed warships.

The French developed the last type of galley, known as the réale, which carried light cannon in the bow. As with later warships, the captain and officers were housed in luxurious quarters in the stern, while the crew lived between-decks as best they could. The anchor-cable locker and ship's storeroom were situated forward and served as the hospital in time of battle. A unique feature of the réale was a large room amidships called the 'tavern', which served both as a sail locker and a wine shop: wine was as necessary to the crew of these galleys as rum was to the later sailors of the 'wooden-walls', for their existence aboard was miserable in the extreme. So low were the bulwarks of these fast but unseaworthy vessels that the oarsmen were often rowing up to their waists in water.

The last galley of this type was built in 1720, for by then it was acknowledged that the light hull-construction which gave the galley its speed also made it vulnerable to the cannon of the more stoutly built warships; in 1684, for example, the guns of the French warship *Le Bon* had smashed an entire fleet of thirty-five galleys.

The French réale. The last of these war galleys was built in 1720.

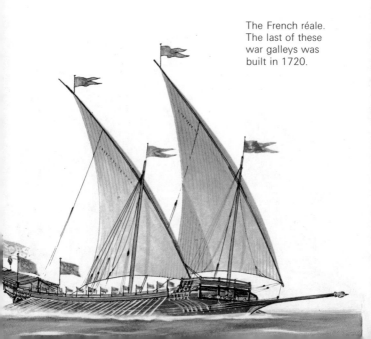

The Mediterranean and Aegean seas were enhanced up to thirty or forty years ago by a multitude of unusually rigged and gaily adorned sailing vessels, bearing equally colourful names. These vessels, which have unfortunately vanished almost without trace before the onset of marine engines and politics, illustrate the incorporation of both Mediterranean and Northern European aspects of ship design and sail plan.

Among the most graceful of these vanished ships was the two-masted Venetian rascona. Equipped with a single steering-oar on the starboard quarter of the long and graceful hull, propelled by two European-type lugsails adorned with gay devices and with a large deck-cabin aft, the rascona was a combination of the basic Mediterranean round-ship and Northern longship, with the emphasis on the latter.

The Genoese vinco was one of the most spectacular of all the traditional-type Mediterranean sailing vessels. The built-up stern and sweep of the hull were similar to those of the Algerian

Venetian rascona

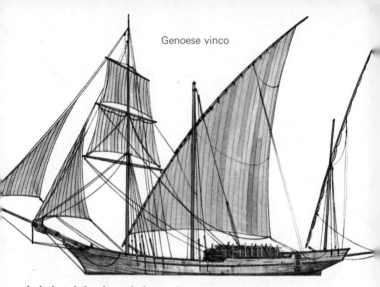

Genoese vinco

chebek, whilst the sail plan and mast rig was a distinct combination of Mediterranean and Northern European concepts. The foremast carried three square sails and yards together with an outer jib, inner jib and foresail stayed to a long bowsprit, complete with 'dolphin striker', after the manner of northern ships. The mainmast and mizzen, on the other hand, carried the traditional lateen sails of the Mediterranean. The mizzen sail was controlled from a 'bumpkin' or short spar extending over the stern – a device still used by the few remaining inshore fishing boats on the Suffolk coast of England.

Maltese sperona

Greek scapho

The single-masted, lateen-rigged Maltese sperona has an unusual projection of the bow reminiscent of the ram of the Greek war galleys, whilst the high rail round the deck probably evolved from the deck screens of plaited osiers used by the early Greek trading ships to protect their cargoes. European influence shows in the centrally mounted rudder, long bowsprit and large triangular foresail.

The Greek scapho was an unusual vessel in that its general appearance was almost completely Northern European. The hull was similar in shape to the open fishing dories used on the coast of North America, and was clinker-built, i.e. with overlapping planks. The huge, gaff-rigged mainsail was further reinforced by a long diagonal spar or sprit, after the manner of the Thames sailing barges – which were known as 'spritties'. The only traditional Mediterranean feature of this somewhat ungainly-looking vessel is the canvas 'dodger' or screen laced to the deck rails.

The Greek sacoleva was an even more striking combination of Northern and Southern innovations than the scapho. It was one of those traditional Mediterranean craft about which relatively little is known. The mainmast raked forward as in the ninth- and tenth-century Mediterranean merchant vessels and carried a gaff-rigged mainsail which, like that of the scapho, was stretched by a diagonal sprit. Above the mainsail was a yard which carried a square sail. The mizzen mast raked aft and carried a lateen sail which was controlled from a 'bumpkin'. At first glance the sacoleva could be taken for a European topsail schooner until closer examination shows the traditional Mediterranean 'round-ship' hull, adapted for greater cargo capacity. An unusual feature is that both masts are almost of the same length, whereas the topsail schooner has a foremast which is much shorter than the mainmast. Finally, where the topsail schooner carries a gaff mainsail and a gaff maintopsail, the sacoleva is rigged with a lateen sail only on the after mast.

The Turkish tchektirme (overleaf) is another interesting combination of Mediterranean and Northern European ship design. The hull was carvel-built, the planks laid edge to edge, in the traditional Mediterranean style. But the gaff-rigged mainsail, foresail, inner jib, outer jib and long, canted bowsprit gave the tchektirme a striking similarity to a nineteenth-century North Sea cutter-rigged sailing trawler.

Greek sacoleva

The single-masted Turkish mahovna, or sailing barge, carried a large lateen sail laced to a long, counter-weighted yard which was slung to a stump mast.

The shape and sheer of the bow are distinctly Egyptian in appearance, being almost identical to the bow of the large, lateen-rigged Nile boom. The long bowsprit holding the fore-sail and jib, on the other hand, gives the forepart of the mahovna a definitely European look. It is unfortunate that the Turks appear to have kept no record of the construction or functions of their earlier, more humble types of traditional sailing craft, though, like the billyboy, hoy, and other quaintly named traditional types of English sailing craft, they seem to have been maritime 'maids of all work'.

Powered vessels have mostly displaced these picturesque and exotically named craft although a few can be found scattered along the ports of the Mediterranean and Aegean Seas. But, like the tan-sailed trawlers and drifters which once thronged the East Coast fishing ports of England, they have been shorn of their sails and reduced to stump masts and diesel or petrol engines.

The single-masted Turkish tchektirme, with its gaff-rigged mainsail, foresail and two jibs

The mahovna, a single-masted
Turkish sailing barge

Spanish and Portuguese vessels

The single-masted, lateen-rigged Spanish tartane (overleaf)
is another example of a basically Mediterranean-type vessel
incorporating innovations from Northern Europe. For, whilst
the stem extending well above the bow follows a Greek
concept, the triangular jib and bowsprit indicate European
influence.

The two-masted, lateen-rigged Spanish felucca bore a
striking resemblance to the Algerian Corsairs' chebek, with its
forward-raking mainmast, extended stem-piece, its 'lute' or
overhanging stern, long bowsprit and big foresail. Indeed, it
is likely that the Spaniards were strongly influenced by the
chebek's speed, seaworthiness and graceful lines. The felucca
of later times is a long, double-ended, or transom-sterned,
open boat, carrying a single forward-raking mast and the
traditional lateen, which is an outstanding example of
Mediterranean sail development. Originally a conventional
square lug-type sail, the lateen had its leading or weather edge

– known as the *luff* – greatly reduced, and the yard thus set at
an angle. The reason for this modification was that whilst the
original type of sail was satisfactory in light airs, it caused the
felucca to bury its bow in the sudden fierce winds of the
Mediterranean.

Like the colourful traditional sailing vessels of the Mediterranean, the Spanish tartane and the felucca have now disappeared in the wake of the marine engine, hastened too by the
Spanish government's disapproving attitude towards the
continuation of traditional wooden sailing vessels.

Typically Mediterranean in rig and form, except for the
clinker-built hull, was the two-masted, lateen-rigged Portuguese Tagus frigata which, as its name suggests, originated on
the River Tagus. Characteristic of this sailing vessel were the
stump masts of equal length; the mizzen mast raking slightly
aft; the extended and ornately decorated stem- and stern-
pieces, and the decorative panels on the bow.

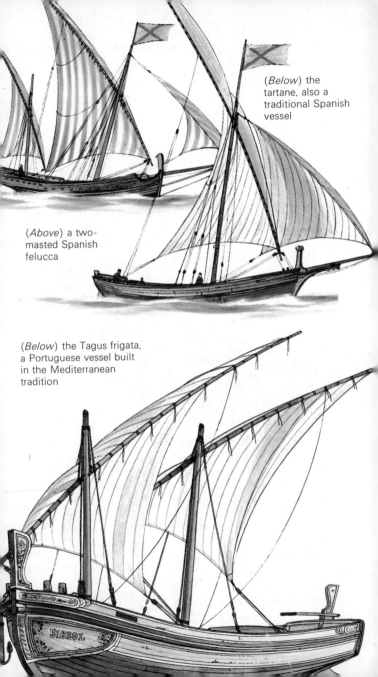

(*Below*) the tartane, also a traditional Spanish vessel

(*Above*) a two-masted Spanish felucca

(*Below*) the Tagus frigata, a Portuguese vessel built in the Mediterranean tradition

51620L

A Portuguese
wine-boat

The Douro wine boat, which carried port down the River Douro to Oporto for maturing, was an extremely primitive craft, yet well designed for its particular function. The hull – distinctly Egyptian in form with a long upward-curving bow and stern (see gaiassa, page 6) – was broad-beamed and of shallow draught, built with the minimum of cross beams in order to facilitate the stowing of wine casks. The Nilotic appearance of this craft was increased by the huge, loose-bellied square sail set on a mast stepped slightly aft, and the tower-like wooden platform from which the boat was steered round the sharp bends of the Douro by means of a ponderous sweep, or oar (projecting to the right of the picture), reminiscent of the sweeps used to manoeuvre the Thames lighters.

The strange-looking Portuguese muletta, used for both drift-net (surface fishing) and trawling (bottom fishing), was, despite its appearance, well designed for its function. The large lateen sail, set on a forward-raking mast and supplemented by a primitive form of double spinnaker, gave the vessel forward movement. The muletta is one of the most interesting sailing vessels in existence, for it incorporates features of the ships of three maritime peoples far removed in place and time: the iron spiked bow was identical to the 'skegg' or 'beard' of a type of armoured Norse longship known as a jarnbardi; the gaily painted *oculi* on the bow were traditionally Mediterranean, and the tub-shaped hull and leeboards were reminiscent of a nineteenth-century Dutch hektjalk.

The Portuguese muletta, a fishing craft of unusual rig. Note the *oculus* on the bow.

Two vessels of
the Ganges: the
patile (*above*)
and the palla

India

The Ganges patile, a large single-masted, lugsail-rigged cargo vessel, is unusual in that it is probably the only clinker-built boat to be found on the River Ganges. An unusual feature, to Western eyes, is the palm-thatched deck-house extending almost the entire length of the vessel and mounted by a bamboo cat-walk, from the after end of which the patile is steered by means of a long-loomed, balanced rudder. The massive blade of this powerful rudder extends well forward of the rudder stock, thus providing the extra control needed when the vessel is heavily laden. The patile is sometimes adorned with *oculi* on the bow.

The single-masted, lugsail-rigged palla, or pulwa, and the mala pansi have upward-curving bows and sterns in the Egyptian manner, and rudders mounted on the port quarter. The hulls of both are carvel-built, and the mast of the mala pansi is stepped in a tall tabernacle which permits it to be lowered aft when the wind fails and paddles must be used. Both craft have the conventional palm-thatched cabin. They are used to ferry market-produce across the Ganges.

The mala pansi, one of the smallest of the Ganges sailing craft

An unconventional but highly efficient craft is the carvel-built balance-board fishing boat of the Palk Strait, between India and Ceylon. Instead of depending on the more usual type of outrigger (see page 47), it has a long plank of heavy palmyra wood which is lashed athwartships and secured each side by a shroud from the mast. In fresh winds the balance-board is run out on the weather side of the boat and given additional support by the lee shroud, which is shifted to the weather side of the board to serve also as a lifeline.

These balance-board boats are lugsail-rigged on one to three masts and they are of shallow draught, with no keel. This shallow draught enables them to feel their way along the maze of shallow, narrow channels amid the offshore mud banks, and

The spectacular kola maram, also known as the 'flying-fish' catamaran

A lugsail-rigged balance-board fishing boat from the Palk Strait

combines with their length and large sail area to make them the swiftest of the traditional Indian sailing craft. They are equipped with a narrow leeboard to counteract the lack of keel and have two thin steering oars manipulated by the feet of the helmsman, who squats on a small deck in the stern.

The most spectacular of all the 'catamarans' (Indian *kattumaran* = tied logs) is the big, seven-log kola maram or 'flying-fish catamaran' of the Coromandel Coast. It consists of seven big logs securely lashed together, narrowed at the bow and having five upward-curving stempieces, which help the craft to skim at speed in pursuit of flying fish. Again, leeboards are lowered to counteract the lack of keel. The fishing season is short, so the crew are forced to spend long periods aboard.

Burma, Thailand and Saigon

From the beginning of history the dense jungles of Burma and Thailand have made the Irawadi, Salween and Mekong Rivers the only means of transport over vast tracts of land. Because of this the native boats and vessels have developed through the centuries from the first crude dugout canoes to large, picturesque and highly specialized sailing craft which nevertheless clearly retain the basic structure of their primitive prototypes.

The hull of the Irawadi rice boat still has the form of the dugout canoe in the underpart, which is built by steaming the frame and then stretching it to the required beam when flexible. The high bulwarks, lofty and ornately carved poop, massive and powerful rudder shipped on the port quarter; the huge, swag-bellied sails, the long, palm-thatched deck-house and the outboard galleries from which the vessel is poled when necessary – all are innovations of the passing centuries. Magnificent carving on the poop forms floral scrolls incorporat-

The picturesque
Irawadi rice-boat

ing the flowers and creepers of the jungle.

The small rua chalom, frequently seen on the waters of Thailand, is a busy 'maid-of-all-work' cargo boat. Characteristic of this single-masted, lugsailed boat, with its bamboo-roofed deck-house and gracefully sheered stem- and stern-posts, are the narrow-bladed rudders, one on each quarter, giving the rua chalom the likeness of an early Mediterranean trading vessel.

The flat-bottomed Thai twako, with its battened lugsails, raking foremast and brightly painted hull adorned with *oculi* on the bow, is, to all intents and purposes, a Chinese junk. Unlike the junk, however, the twako is steered by a rudder shipped conventionally to the stern post, instead of the junk-type rudder which passes through a rudder trunk in the poop. The ghe ca vom (overleaf), a long, narrow river-boat of Saigon, has a distinctly Egyptian appearance, strengthened by the short lengths of timber of the hull. The single mast, which is stepped well forward, carries an unusual sail, a combination of Oriental lugsail and Occidental gaff sail. A small bamboo deck-house shelters the crew, and the

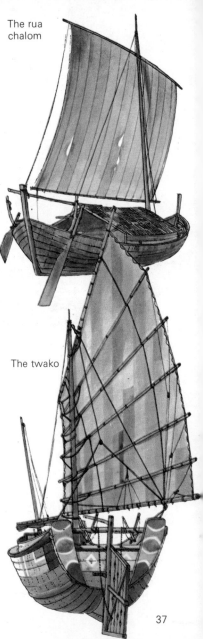

The rua chalom

The twako

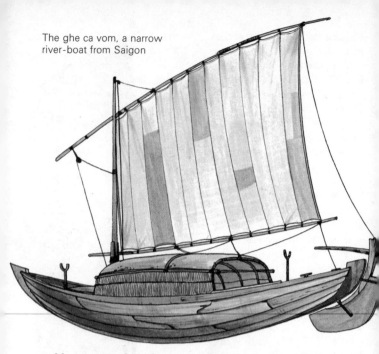
The ghe ca vom, a narrow river-boat from Saigon

rudder, mounted on the stern-post, curves gracefully beneath the hull, thus giving greater purchase and control.

The ghe luoi rung is a mixture of East and West. This picturesque boat has a shallow, spoon-shaped, gaily painted, carvel-built hull, bearing a large *oculus* on each bow – all features which recall the model funeral ships found in Egyptian tombs. But the three upright masts are stayed, European fashion, by dead-eyes secured to chain-plates, and the mainmast is powerfully stayed to a bow bearing a miniature figurehead. Most astonishing of all is the sail plan, known as the Gunter rig – once esteemed in the British Royal Navy for its smart appearance and ease of handling. The rudder is like that of the ghe ca vom. The *oculus* symbolized the watchful and protective eye of the ancient Egyptian god Horus. The Stone Age mariners of Crete also adopted this symbol to depict the eyes of their ancient mother-goddess Rhea, protectress of sailors (among other things). Eventually the *oculi* were adopted by the Phoenicians, the Greeks, the Romans and even by the

Portuguese, whose boats still bear them. The belief in the benign and watchful ship-deity, eternally alert for dangers seen through the symbolic eyes, spread to Africa and Asia: the vessels of Zanzibar have *oculi* on bow and stern; the Chinese adopted three forms, 'The Dragon's Eye', 'The Tadpole Eye' and 'The Phoenix Eye'.

This far-reaching cult has become very complex. If the crew are Hindu or Buddhist their craft will most likely be adorned with *oculi*. Islam, however, forbids the practice.

The ghe luoi rung, its bow adorned with *oculi*. Sailors still speak of the forepart as the 'eyes' of a ship.

China

The junk – perhaps the oldest traditional type of sailing vessel in existence – has largely retained its original shape. The hull has a short bow and stern and no keel; it probably developed from a primitive form of double canoe.

The Hoangho Ch'uan, or Yellow River junk, was the simplest in form, and has been called 'a floating packing crate'. Built of iron-clamped planks of Tung Liu Mu wood, it was divided into three more or less watertight compartments and had a cargo capacity of about twenty tons.

The Pechili trading junk, found near Singapore until 1910, with its crew of twenty to thirty men, is regarded as the oldest type of Chinese sea-junk. This vessel – flat-bottomed to permit running aground on sandbanks without damage – was of impressive dimensions: 140–180 feet overall, with a beam of 20 to 30 feet and a cargo capacity of up to 400 tons.

The Pechili trader, built in Shanghai to trade between Yinghow, Shanghai and the other ports of Kiangsi and Chekiang, was unique in the stepping of its masts. The foremast was stepped outboard on the port side; the two mainmasts and mizzen were stepped in line. Well aft on the port side, an

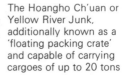

The Hoangho Ch'uan or Yellow River Junk, additionally known as a 'floating packing crate' and capable of carrying cargoes of up to 20 tons

The Pechili trading junk

auxiliary mizzen was stepped just clear of the tiller and used to bring the ship about when tacking.

In addition to the large lugsails, a staysail was frequently set between the two mainmasts and – most unusual in a junk – a large topsail was set to give greater way to the unwieldy vessel in light airs. A long deck-house aft provided shelter for the crew, whilst an extended 'lute-stern' type of after-deck provided working space for the handling of the mizzen sails. Decorations were few.

41

The three-masted, lugsail-rigged Foochow pole junk was once a common sight off the coast of China, with its deck cargo of poles. It was a lumbering vessel with a cargo capacity of 200–400 tons, and was generally reinforced with thin iron plating imported from British scrap merchants: it was not unusual to see a junk bearing an advertisement for 'Wright's Coal Tar Soap'.

The sails were the conventional battened lugsail of heavy white or brown canvas; decoration varied according to the home port. The crew of twenty to thirty men lived aft in a big deck-house under the protection of the ship's deity, or joss.

Their massive hardwood frames, divided into watertight thwartship compartments every eight feet, and fore-and-aft compartments every four feet, made these cumbersome craft

The Foochow pole junk

The Chinese lorcha, first built in Macao in 1843

eminently seaworthy; the pole junk *Keying*, commanded by Captain Kellet, sailed from Hong Kong via the Cape of Good Hope to London in 1848. In 1908 the *Whangho* sailed from Hong Kong to Sydney, and in 1912 the *Ningpo* made a voyage from Shanghai to San Francisco.

The Chinese lorcha was an unusual vessel – a hybrid, like the polacca-chebek. The first lorchas were built by the Portuguese at Macao in 1843 to fight the pirates which swarmed the China seas and rivers. They had Chinese sail rigs and flat-bottomed westernized hulls built of teak and camphor wood. In 1847, seven lorchas cleaned out the pirate nests of the Ningpo area. After this the lorchas were of no further use to the Portuguese, who sold them. Thus these specialized vessels – later copied by the Chinese – fell into the hands of gun-runners and smugglers. Just before the breed declined, a Chinese lorcha, the *Arrow*, was instrumental in sparking off the Sino-British war of 1857–60. Until about 1865 lorchas were easily identified by their paintwork: rusty red, with a bright yellow poop and forecastle and a white deck-house.

Japan and Formosa

It is an astonishing anomaly to find that the Japanese – a true maritime people – should have but one type of junk and that of poor design and performance.

It was a beamy, heavily built, lugsail-rigged vessel, with two, or three masts. It had, however, an inherent, and dangerous, defect: the open well of the stern, built to permit the raising and lowering of the rudder, rendered the vessel very liable to be pooped, that is, swamped by a wave breaking over the stern. Most surprising of all, the side galleries and artemon-like foremast were almost identical to those of the early Roman corn ships.

The heavy surf of the east coast of Formosa has caused the evolution of a type of sailing raft which is considered to be the most advanced of this class of sailing transport. The Taiwan raft is built of large bamboos, curving upwards at each side and at the bow. The mast is a large stem of bamboo and the matting sail the traditional type of Chinese sail, supported by

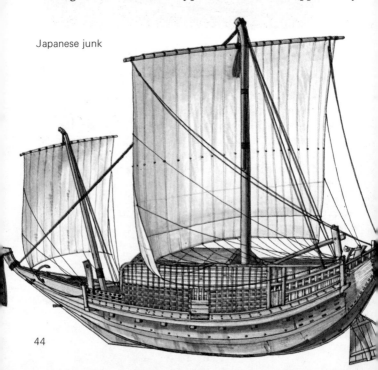

Japanese junk

The Taiwan raft, built to weather the heavy surf off the east coast of Formosa

cross battens. To prevent the craft making leeway when under sail the crew push narrow boards down between the bamboo stems of the hull.

This was a Chinese innovation from which the drop-keel or centre-board has been developed. In the centre of the raft is a large wooden tub with a plank seat on which passengers sit to keep their feet dry. In addition to the sail, the raft is equipped with four large, self-feathering oars which are known as 'yulohs' and which are worked from crutches, one at each corner of the raft.

The self-feathering action of the yulohs is obtained by the blade of the oar being at a slight angle to the loom or handle. This obviates the necessity of the oarsman turning the blade of his oar when it leaves the water.

Indonesia

In times past, the two-masted flying-prau or prahu of Java, which originated in Malaya, was a sight all voyagers in the Java Sea feared: she carried heavy swivel guns fore-and-aft and was usually a pirate ship.

The flying-prau was fifty feet long and had a fourteen-foot beam. She was a hybrid, for her high poop and long bowsprit, with conventional triangular jib, were Western innovations; while the two steering oars (one on each quarter), the outboard galleries and the peculiar curve of the masthead showed Mediterranean influence. The bipod mast and the frameless, teak-planked hull supported by cross-beams, inserted after the hull was built, are identical to those of traditional early Egyptian craft.

The sail-plan of the flying-prau altered little over the centuries, as illustrated by the ship carvings of Boro-Badur, Java, which were executed nearly a thousand years ago. A characteristic of this rakish craft was the primitive but effective way in which the crew kept their food from rats and other vermin that inevitably haunted the prau: they just slung their rations from the mast in a large earthenware pot.

The prau bedang, from Madura, near Java, is a long, two-masted craft with double outriggers. Steered by a single oar, the prau bedang is higher in the stern than the bow, which

The flying-prau or prahu from Java

The prau bedang from Madura, equipped with double outriggers

projects forward in the form of a ram. The mast-plan resembles that of a two-masted schooner, with the mainmast stepped near the stern and the shorter foremast stepped well forward. The triangular sails, with the head laced to a yard and the foot laced to a boom, appear to be a hybrid form of lug-lateen.

In complete contrast to the long prau bedang, the two-masted, carvel-built, cargo-carrying prau mayang is of the 'round-ship' form. Steered by an oar from the port quarter, this craft carries a large lug-lateen type of sail on the mainmast, which is stepped well forward. The long bowsprit and triangular fore-staysail show marked Western influence. A large cabin, open at the stern, shelters crew and cargo.

The prau mayang, a cargo
vessel built on
'round-ship' lines

47

The caracor, a double outrigger indigenous to the waters of New Guinea, the Celebes, Borneo and Java, has stem- and stern-posts extended somewhat in the manner of a Norse longship. The tripod mast carries a large lug-lateen type of sail, the head laced to a long yard and the foot to a long boom, and the craft is steered by an oar shipped on the port quarter.

Because of its speed and general handiness the caracor was used by the Dutch as a patrol boat until comparatively recently.

Like the flying-prau of Java, the tripod-masted Moro outrigger boat of the Sulu Sea was always given a wide berth, for it was frequently manned by Moro head-hunters. The hull of this primitive but dangerous craft consisted of a simple dugout canoe balanced by a single heavy outrigger to port. The tripod mast carried a very large sail of the lug-lateen type, which gave the outrigger tremendous speed when it was sailing with a fair wind.

The double-outrigger caracor, a native Indonesian craft

The primitive Moro outrigger, often manned by head-hunters

The South Pacific

The dugout canoe is the most primitive and widely-spread of all forms of water transport, being used by prehistoric man all over the world. In Britain, for example, two dugout canoes were found when the Ribble Docks were being dug at Preston. These dugout canoes were suitable logs, hollowed out by fire or stone axes; in the South Pacific axes made from the hard shell of the tridacna, or giant clam, were used.

The New Guinea lakatoi (overleaf) consists of three or more large dugout canoes formed into a single craft by passing stout beams through them. A solid bamboo platform is then lashed to the completed hull, whilst two masts – stepped close together amidships – are rigged with odd sails which are shaped like the claws of a giant lobster.

These unusual craft – which show neither oriental nor occidental influence – are approximately sixty feet overall, with a beam of fifty feet; thus the lakatoi resembles a sailing raft rather than a true boat. It is stable but unwieldy, requiring four cumbersome paddles, pivoted at the stern, to steer it. Principally used by the Papuans of Port Moresby for trading and for ceremonial races, the craft were decorated with tassels and garlands of leaves and carried a troupe of dancing girls at the fore end. The lakatoi was large enough to carry up to thirty people on a long coastal voyage.

The Tongan calie was a double canoe, one canoe shorter than the other, and was used for fishing and carrying goods, passengers and raiding parties. It consisted of two canoes lashed together by large beams which supported a platform holding the mast and deck-house. Extra free-board was achieved by raising the sides of the canoes by means of planks sewn on with palm-fibre twine. The foreward-raking

A triple-hulled, two-masted New Guinea lakatoi, with its curious, claw-shaped sails

A Hawaiian double canoe

mast, stayed fore-and-aft, was rigged with a sail of the lug-lateen type, whilst the calie was steered by paddles from both sides.

The double canoe – often mistakenly called a cata-maran – originated in the South Pacific. Two types of this craft were used, one with canoes of equal length, the other – like the calie – with canoes of different lengths.

These fast and handy craft, often highly decorated and ornamented with intricate carvings and designs of inlaid tridacna shell and pearl shell, were to be found in the waters of Tonga, Samoa, the Low Archipelago and New Zealand. Such was the Tongan's skill as shipwrights that they were frequently employed by other South Pacific peoples as shipbuilders.

The Tongan calie

The ornate waka taua, a dugout war canoe built by the Maoris

For a period covering a thousand years the Maoris, a mixed Polynesian and Melanesian people, set out on great trans-Pacific migrations to New Zealand. The type of vessel they used was an enormous double canoe called a tainui. They were over seventy feet long and were driven on their formidable voyages by means of two claw-shaped sails, similar to those of the lakatoi, supported on lofty bipod masts. On the massive cross-beams which joined the two huge canoes of the hull, a stout platform was built to hold a large cabin, which was the accommodation of the chief and his men, whilst the women-folk lived in one of the canoes. The food supplies for the migrants were carried in deep holds. The tainui was remarkable for the huge, blade-shaped decorations of the stern which were twenty feet high and ornamented with the traditional spiral motif of the Maoris. Like the Tongan calie, the Maori tainui was given additional free-board by means of extra planking sewn on with palm-fibre twine.

When the sea-weary Maoris reached New Zealand they were quick to utilize the huge Kauri pine trees to build their magnificent war canoe, the waka taua, the most ornate of all the traditional craft of the Pacific Ocean. Propelled both by paddles and by a highly betasselled sail in the form of an inverted triangle, the waka taua was a single dugout canoe, seventy feet long and with a beam of only five feet – dimensions which gave this handsome craft tremendous speed.

Like the tainui, the waka taua carried a tall, blade-shaped decoration at the stern, whilst the ornately carved bow bore the figure of a fearsome mythical creature called the 'Manaia' – its tongue protruding in the traditional war grimace of the fierce Maori warriors.

African craft
The mtepi, of the Lamu Archipelago off the coast of Kenya, was a single-masted, matting-sailed vessel originally used for carrying firewood and mangrove poles to Zanzibar.

In general appearance the mtepi resembled an Arab dhow,

The tainui, used by the Maoris on their trans-Pacific migrations

The mtepi, a matting-sailed vessel from the coast of Kenya

with its sharply-raking bow and stern and gaily adorned rudder. The hull, however, was built with planks sewn together with coir twine and caulked from inboard by coir fibres hammered into the seams and then covered with bands of coir fibre and palm-leaf stalks.

When the hull was completed it was reinforced by rib frames which were lashed inside through holes bored in the planking and then plugged by wooden stoppers. Accommodation for the crew was a palm-thatched cabin aft.

The stem- and stern-posts of this unusual vessel were built up with blocks of wood, arranged to overlap – thus giving the necessary rake – and then pinned into position by trenails. This method of ship construction was used by countries where suitable wood for shipbuilding was scarce and could well have been inherited from the ancient Egyptians.

Characteristic of this East African craft were the tassels of palm fibre and the three gaily coloured flags adorning the beak-like bow, which in some instances also bore a figurehead and *oculi*. The inherent weakness of the mtepi lay in the piecemeal construction of the stem and stern and in the large, unwieldy sail, which made the vessel awkward to handle except in fair winds.

The single-outrigger canoe is essentially a type of coastal craft used for its lightness and ease of handling amongst islands where surf and sudden squalls are encountered. Under such conditions the double-outrigger canoe is unsuitable, owing to the fact that the double outrigger can constitute a positive danger when the craft is thrown on its beam ends by a sudden squall or surf and the lee outrigger is suddenly submerged.

Under these conditions the drag of the lee outrigger makes steering difficult and could cause enough strain to destroy the craft. Typical of the single outrigger canoe is the sakalavan of Madagascar. The hull of this fishing canoe is a narrow dugout with a thwartship frame which carries the outrigger and the midship platform from which the frail but fast and seaworthy craft is steered by means of a paddle.

The single-outrigger
sakalavan of Madagascar

A sailing balsa made of reed bundles, from Lake Titicaca, Peru

South American craft

The largest Peruvian sailing balsas were used until recently for carrying livestock and passengers, and for fishing, on Lake Titicaca. They were double-ended, with a crew of two, and capable of carrying up to twelve people. The hull was constructed of two spirally-bound reed bundles, twenty feet long, tapered and curved to form the bow and stern. Two smaller bundles were then lashed along each side to provide the necessary free-board. The bamboo masts – either single or bipod – were shipped so that they could be lowered forward when not in use. The sail, woven of totoa matting, laced to a bamboo yard and boom and reinforced by four light bamboo battens, was rigged on the after side of the mast. The balsas last for two to three months only, after which the reeds and lashings rot and fall to pieces.

The jangada, a log-built sailing raft used by fishermen in Brazil

The jangada is a primitive but specialized raft used by Brazilian fishermen. The rectangular dish-shaped hull consists of several lightwood logs, pinned together with long wooden dowels. The sail is rigged on a free sprit, as on a spritsail barge. On larger jangadas accommodation is a thatched cabin built on a platform aft, behind which is the crutch into which the mast is lowered when not in use. To offset the leeway due to its shallow draught, the jangada carries a centre keel housed in a hardwood casing just aft of the mast, and a long, narrow-bladed rudder-cum-steering oar is also used.

SAILING VESSELS OF NORTHERN EUROPE

Skin boats of Ireland and the Arctic

These primitive craft were built by stretching ox-hides over sewn, or cloven, withe frames. They, like the Chinese junk, have altered little over the centuries – except that in more recent times the ox-hide covering was replaced by tarred calico. A small gold model of a curragh is part of the Broyghter Treasure Hoard, dated 200 BC. The original was probably forty feet long, with a large ox-hide lug-type sail rigged to a rough tree-trunk mast and steered by a heavy oar rigged on the port quarter. The anchor – 'killick' – was a long, heavy stone to which two wooden flukes were lashed.

Owing to its seaworthiness, lightness and speed, the seagoing sailing curragh was frequently used by the early Irish invaders of Britain. Chief of these was King Niall of the Nine Hostages, who ruled Ireland AD 379–405. He invaded Wales with such success that he was able to establish Irish colonies there. Later, in 519, St Brendan the Navigator left Ireland in a similar craft on a five-year voyage. Legend tells that he reached Iceland, and even North America.

The skin umiak of the Eskimos was used for whale hunting, but as this gradually ceased, it became an all-purpose craft, sometimes used for hunting but more often for carrying families and goods to new homes when necessary.

The frame was very much the same as one of a conventional carvel-built boat, except that it was fastened with skin thongs and was built of driftwood. It was covered with some fifteen to twenty sealskins, sewn into sections by Eskimo women, then stretched and secured inboard by thongs to the stringers beneath the gunwales. The umiak was approximately thirty feet long with a beam of five to six feet. The mast carried a lug-type sail of reindeer skin (in later years blue or white cotton drill was used). The boat carried several pairs of oars, a long steering oar and a bailer. The umiak carried specialized equipment of carved and ornamented walrus ivory – such as boat fittings, harpoon rests, lance toggles, snow and ice beaters for clearing the boat, clothing and strings of good-luck charms.

The Irish curragh

Norse longships

The Norwegian Vikings jealously claimed the name 'Northmen' for themselves, but ethnically the term is much broader. It embraces all the Scandinavian peoples, the Saxons, Jutes and Angles, the Slavonic Wends of the Baltic coast, the Norse settlers of Iceland, the Germanic Franks, the Finns and Russians, the Enskirmenn or English, the Irskirmenn or Irish, and many others. Thus, as in the Southern hemisphere, the ship development of the North was a multi-racial affair. The Northern seamen, faced with the fury of winter winds and waves and racing tides unknown in the Mediterranean, built their ships accordingly: even today the Norse longship is regarded by experts as the most seaworthy type of basic sailing vessel ever evolved.

Whilst the peoples of the East and the Mediterranean left comparatively little ship lore to posterity, the Northmen left much: stone carvings and grave finds tell us much about how they built their ships; they even buried their dead in ships, several of which have been unearthed.

In 1939 the remains of a Saxon longship were unearthed at Sutton Hoo, near Woodbridge, Suffolk. Although no wood was found, the dimensions of the Sutton Hoo Ship could be calculated from the position of the iron nails still remaining. It was considered the most important ship find in the northern hemisphere because of the splendid treasures it contained. Chief of these (now on display in the British Museum) was a massive sword with a solid gold jewel-encrusted hilt and a unique fibula of gold, which indicated that this may have been the memorial of Aethelhere, a Saxon king of East Anglia.

The Sutton Hoo Ship,
length 84ft, beam 14ft

The Gokstad Ship, built about a thousand years ago; length 77ft, beam 17ft. Above it is the *Hugin*, a 20th-century version of a Viking snekja.

Nevertheless, the discovery in 1880 of the twenty-ton, oak-built Gokstad Ship near Sandjefiord, Norway, was of equally great significance. For, where the Sutton Hoo Ship had rotted completely, the Gokstad Ship had been buried in blue clay which had preserved it almost intact for a thousand years. Built approximately three centuries after the Sutton Hoo Ship, the Gokstad Ship had a sepulchral chamber containing a carved wooden bier on which lay the remains of a Norse sea warrior with a massive axe, iron plates and buckles of his war harness, a large chest which served as the ship's armoury, and items of wood and iron ship chandlery. Along each bulwark of the ship were thirty-two wooden shields, alternately coloured black and yellow, whilst each oar-port was sealed with a wooden disc or deadlight to keep the water out when the ship was heeling under sail.

A replica very similar to the Gokstad Ship can be seen at Pegwell Bay near Ramsgate, Kent. This ship, the *Hugin*, was built of oak at Frederikssund near Copenhagen, and in 1949, with a crew of fifty-three men dressed as Vikings, she crossed from Esbjerg to the Kent coast in two weeks. The 'Vikings' brought gifts of silver and amber to commemorate their ancestors. The *Hugin*, built from records at Greenwich and Copenhagen, was an average-sized Viking ship known as a snekja or 'snake', seventy-one feet overall with a beam of eighteen feet, which could carry up to 150 men. The biggest longships, known collectively as *herskips* – meaning 'hosts of war' – and individually as *drekis*, or 'dragons', were infinitely more formidable in size and crew. The saga of King Olaf Trygvasson who ruled Norway a thousand years ago, tells of such a ship – the *Ormrinn Langi* or 'Long Serpent': 'King Olaf had a large ship built at Hladhamrar. It was one hundred and eighty feet long with a beam exceeding thirty-eight feet and with stem- and stern-posts rising fifteen feet above the water. Thorberg Skarfhogg was the stemsmith (shipwright). Besides being long and broad, the ship had high bulwarks and massive timbers and all men said that they had never seen such a fine or large longship. Early one morning the King and Thorberg went to look at the ship and found great cuts in both bulwarks. Then the King was greatly angered and said that if he knew the man that had spoiled the ship then that man should die, but not easily. But that the man who told him of the culprit's name should have a great reward. Then said Thorberg: "I can tell you, king, who did this thing." "Then tell it!" said the King. "I have done it," said Thorberg. "Then," said the King, "Thou shalt repair it so that it is as good as before – or lose thy life!" Then Thorberg took his axe and shaped one side of the ship so that the cuts had disappeared and everyone said that the ship was better on that side even than before. Then the King asked Thorberg to do the same on the other side, and when it was done thanked him well.'

The *Long Serpent* was said to have been the finest and costliest longship ever built in Norway and had a total complement of 700 men. The biggest longship known in history was Knut (King Canute) the Great's *Great Dragon* which was 300 feet overall, manned by 120 oarsmen and carried a total complement of approximately one thousand. *Leidangr* was a highly organized system of ship levy which enabled the Norsemen to assemble the largest fleets of any maritime people. The two largest of these fleets, totalling from five to six thousand longships, were engaged in the battle of Bravoll, Eastern Gautland, in AD 700.

Norse naval tactics – and their ships – were highly developed. For example, they used a type of 'armoured cruiser' known as a jarnbardi. This was a large, reinforced longship armoured above the water line with iron plates and carrying a deadly iron-spiked skegg or 'beard' on the bow, for ramming. Such a formidable and unconventional vessel, commanded by Eric Jarl, son of Hakon Jarl who ruled Norway AD 965–995, did

The Oseberg Ship, a fine example of a Viking longship

great execution at the bloody battles of Swold and Jomsvikings.

The Norsemen used as many as 3,000 ships, and supply-vessels were essential: capacious vistabrydings (ships of burden) carried food, livestock, weapons and ammunition, and smiths and forges for repair work at sea. The hepiskuta or 'running ship' carried dispatches. The cargo ship (kaup skip) was greater in beam and depth than the longship, carried no shields on its rails, lacked the 'war girdle', (a massive hawser used to strengthen the hulls of warships) and had no pennants or dragons' heads. Such a ship is described in Egil's Saga:

'Thorolf had a large seagoing ship which was most carefully built and painted all over above the water line. It had a sail of red and blue stripes and all the rigging was very elaborate. This ship Thorolf made ready and ordered his men-servants to go with it. He put on board dried fish, skins, tallow and furs from the mountains – all of great value. Thorolf set the ship westward to buy woollen cloth and other goods he needed. They went southward and then out to sea. When they arrived in England they found a good market, loaded the ship with wheat, honey, wines and cloth and returned in the autumn with fair winds.'

The Norsemen traded to all ports of Western Europe, up the Tigris and Euphrates, and in the Mediterranean and Adriatic Seas; they also sailed to the Black Sea and penetrated by caravan to the heart of Russia.

The Norse kaup skip, a large, seagoing cargo vessel

The Kalmar Boat, length 36ft, beam 15ft

By the Middle Ages, however, the magnificent longships of the Northmen had lost their striking lines, and had come more and more to resemble the Mediterranean 'round ship'. A good example of this type of vessel is the thirteenth-century Kalmar Boat, discovered with many other sunken vessels dating to the seventeenth century in the bay of Kalmar Castle, Sweden, when it was drained between 1932–4.

The oak, clinker-built hull of the Kalmar Boat, when compared to the earlier longships, is disproportionately broad, having a beam of fifteen feet to an overall length of thirty-six feet. This short, rigid, stoutly beamed vessel, decked-in fore-and-aft and driven by a mainsail of 270 square feet, on a sturdy mast stepped amidships, was the prototype of the nineteenth-century English luggers described overleaf.

The nineteenth-century luggers and galleys of Kent and Sussex and the great beach yawls of the east coast all took their

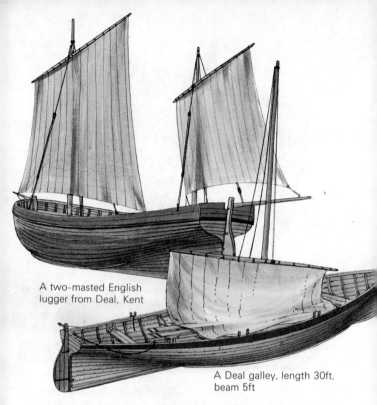

A two-masted English lugger from Deal, Kent

A Deal galley, length 30ft, beam 5ft

lines from much older Norse ships. The most famous luggers were from Deal, Kent – notorious as a smuggling town. When smuggling no longer paid, their owners turned to 'hovelling' – anything from salvaging a wreck to looking for ships to pilot in the Channel. Later luggers were up to forty feet overall, two-masted, lugsail-rigged, and carried seven or eight men, who lived in a cramped cabin forward. In February 1866, the Deal lugger *England's Glory* launched off into the teeth of a 'sou'-westerly buster' to the Goodwins and salvaged the tea-cargo of the *Iron Crown*. It was a feat of supreme seamanship and daring which earned the crew £7,000 in salvage money. The last lugger was sold in 1925 for a mere £2.10.0.

The Deal galleys were often used for life-saving. Driven by a huge lugsail, they also had five rowing thwarts, and were steered by oar as well as by rudder when under sail. Owing to their narrow beam, shallow draught and huge sail, they required nearly half a ton of ballast which had to be quickly shifted to the weather side at each change of tack. Two of these magnificent boats still exist at Deal; they are perhaps the most spectacular and interesting of the remaining sailing craft of Britain.

The East Coast yawl (Norse *yol* = a double-ended, clinker-built boat) was very like the Gokstad Ship. The two-masted, lugsail-rigged yawls were usually up to sixty feet long and manned by some thirty men; they were very fast, and saved thousands of lives. The biggest of these was the mighty *Reindeer* of Great Yarmouth, sixty-nine feet long and capable of sixteen knots. In 1854 her crew challenged the schooner *America* (see page 117) to a race in the North Sea, but the Americans declined the challenge. On 3 April 1814 the famous yawl *Jubilee* of Southwold, Suffolk, raced another yawl to a salvage job, cutting her rival clean in two, probably on purpose for her crew were a 'bold, artful, surly, savage race.' Only a few weeks before the same crew had retaken an English brig from the French and captured a French war lugger!

An East Coast yawl, built on similar lines to the Gokstad Ship and used for rescue work

The Humber keel, a heavy, single-masted barge

A Norfolk wherry, length 50–60ft, beam 10–12ft, draught 2–3ft

Sailing barges

The Humber keel carried general cargo on the Yorkshire Ouse and Humber; it was a single-masted barge with a huge square-sail, and a square topsail for use in fair winds. Bluff in bow and stern and equipped with heavy leeboards, the cumbersome keel was worked by two men. Surprisingly, it was a remote descendant of the Norse longship, like a war-horse which the changing centuries had bred into a cart-horse.

The Norfolk wherry – or keel – was a general cargo carrier on the shallow and labyrinthine waterways of Norfolk. The first was recorded in 1706. A giant, 100-foot wherry with a cargo capacity of eighty-one tons was built around 1890. Normally the capacity was between twenty and twenty-five tons, the hold itself occupied all but a twentieth of the barge's length and was covered with removable two-foot sections of hatch. The remaining space was the wherryman's cabin, which held only a small coal stove, two bunks and two small wooden lockers. Cargo capacity was 20–25 tons, and included stone, coal, crops, timber and cattle cake.

The forty-foot mast – stepped well forward in a tabernacle – was counter-balanced with one and a half tons of lead to permit lowering at bridges. The huge, tanned canvas mainsail was loose-footed but laced to a heavy gaff.

Despite its cumbersome appearance, the wherry could sail surprisingly close to the wind. When a 'dead muzzler' or head wind prevailed, the wherry had to be poled along by means of a heavy quant, a massive pole, eighteen to twenty feet long, with a steel fork at one end and a 'bot' or shoulder-rest at the other. The Norfolk wherrymen needed their famous strength, for 'quanting' meant setting one's shoulder to the 'bot' and walking the length of the wherry, pushing against wind and tide for mile upon mile.

A famous bygone wherryman was George Applegate of Potter Heigham, Norfolk. He could leave Potter Heigham with a fully-loaded wherry at ten o'clock and arrive at Great Yarmouth the same evening, a distance of twenty miles – very often in the teeth of a gale. In their heyday as many as sixteen wherries at a time could be seen loading and discharging at Potter Heigham. In 1950 there were only six wherries in Norfolk, all but one being power-driven.

Thames barges

The true round-bowed Thames sailing barge did not develop until the 1830s. Till then barges were tub-like craft called 'swim headers', i.e. built with an overhanging bow like a present-day Thames lighter. They became the most highly specialized and efficient cargo-carriers ever evolved. Only the wind and two men were required to move a vessel carrying up to 120 tons of cargo. Shaped like a wooden pencil box but chined (curved) at the bilges, they had a draught of six to seven feet when loaded; unloaded they drew a mere two feet and were said to be 'able to sail over a heavy dew' Their flat bottoms and massive strength enabled them to load and discharge on tidal flats, squat happily on shoals and sandbanks, and even be driven on to a lee shore in an emergency.

The most familiar barge rig was the spritsail used by the 'spritties'. It was an enormous tanned canvas mainsail, stretched diagonally by a heavy spar or sprit; its weight was taken by a strong sling called a 'stanliff', whilst the peak was supported by a heavy rope at the head of the mainsail, and the

The shallow-draught, spritsail-rigged Thames sailing barge, said to be able to 'sail over a heavy dew'; length 80ft, beam 18ft

The 'boomie', a ketch-rigged Channel barge

entire spar steadied by rope guys known as 'vangs'. The forward-raking topmast carried a large topsail laced to a short yard called the 'tops'l stick'. The mainmast also supported a large foresail and, for use in light airs, a topmast staysail. The mizzenmast, stepped well aft, carried a sail with both sprit and boom, the sheet of the latter being rove through a block on the rudder. This simple but highly effective arrangement made the barge extremely nimble in going about, for helm and mizzen moved simultaneously.

Instead of lowering and reefing the sails in a squall, the crew merely lowered them partially – known as 'rucking'. The sea-going 'boomie' had a capacity of up to 300 tons and carried an additional jib. A 'stumpie' was a smaller barge without a topsail. All barges carried winch-operated lee-boards.

WARSHIPS (1200–1820)

European developments

The sailing craft of Northern Europe became shorter in proportion to beam during the Middle Ages. The stern-mounted rudder probably first appeared in the twelfth century (one is carved on the font of Winchester Cathedral). By the early 1200s European ships had changed radically. Forecastles and after-castles were being built at bow and stern. The mainmast now had a topcastle – forerunner of the fighting tops of the massive 'wooden-walls' – from which iron bars and quicklime were hurled. Thwartship beams now protruded through the planking, the ends secured by strong wooden pegs. And for the first time in history the square mainsail had reef points for shortening sail in heavy weather.

A 14th-century cog, length 90ft, beam 24ft

During the fourteenth century the cog appeared, a single-masted, sweep-propelled vessel some ninety feet long, with a ten-foot draught. It was strong, clumsy and completely decked-in. The mast was equipped with ratlines secured to chain-plates, to enable the crew to reach the topcastle.

The carrack, which followed the cog, had two to four masts and a capacity of 200–600 tons – a rating based on the tuns of wine carried. It was distinguished by its overhanging forecastle and aftercastle and the 'bonaventure' mast stepped aft of the mizzen mast. A square spritsail on the bowsprit was used to steady the ship's head; fore- and mainmasts were square-rigged, the mizzenmast and bonaventure lateen-rigged.

The carrack reached its peak in Genoa and Venice. History's most famous carrack was Columbus's *Santa Maria*: she was approximately eighty feet overall, with a beam of some twenty-six feet and driven by some 3,500 square feet of canvas.

The carrack, length
80–100ft, beam
25–35ft

A Portuguese caravel

The caravel, of Portuguese origin, was a two- or three-masted, shallow-draught vessel, swifter and more graceful than the carrack, with two distinct sail rigs. The *caravela latina* was lateen-rigged on all masts; the *caravela redonda* was fully square-rigged or both square- and lateen-rigged.

Used largely for coastal work, caravels played an important part in maritime history, for Henry the Navigator, of Portugal, used them at the beginning of the fifteenth century to open up the trade routes to India. *Santa Clara* (called *Niña* after her captain Juan Niño), which accompanied the *Santa Maria* to America, was of some sixty tons, seventy feet overall, with a twenty-four-foot beam and a draught of six feet. She started as a *caravela latina* but Columbus found this rig unsuitable for the existing winds and converted her to a *caravela redonda* in the

Canary Islands. This was done by stepping the raking main-mast well forward in a vertical position and strengthening it by means of a forestay to a bowsprit. The long lateen yards were cut down to square-rigged yards and the suit of lateen sails recut to fit them.

By the end of the fifteenth century ships were reaching out into the Atlantic: the Mediterranean oared galley was no match for this stormy ocean, and lacked carrying capacity. Thus the galleasse, a type of oared frigate, came into existence. They carried the first cannon to fire *through* gun-ports instead of over them (*en barbette*). The galleasse vanished in the eighteenth century, a period when it resembled a gracefully sheered, top-sail rigged ketch.

The galleasse, a type of oared frigate; a number of these ships sailed with the Armada

During the sixteenth century ships increased greatly in size and armament, the largest being *Henry Grâce à Dieu* – known as *Great Harry* – built by Henry VIII of England in 1514 to meet the growing threat of Spain. This towering, four-masted warship of over one thousand tons was the first vessel known ever to carry topgallant masts on fore, main and mizzen masts, together with a topmast on the bonaventure. Rebuilt between 1536 and 1539 *Great Harry* was the most advanced warship of her time. She had a formidable armament – 21 heavy bronze cannon and 130 medium-sized iron cannon. Her crew were armed with a variety of muskets and grenades. *Great Harry* was more a fortress than a ship, for soldiers were more numerous and important than sailors, then considered mere lackeys.

The *Henry Grâce à Dieu*, a massive warship armed with 151 cannon

The galleon or 'Great Ship', probably of Spanish origin and adapted by other countries, was a new type of vessel built to replace the carrack.

Her hull was more slender and graceful, with the forecastle no longer overhanging the bow but built behind a ram-like projection called the beak head which housed the crew's toilets – hence the modern sailors' term 'heads'.

Steering was now controlled by means of the whipstaff – a vertical extension of the tiller which moved on roller bearings in the 'steersman's hutch', a small cabin sunk in the poop deck. The galleon's waist lacked bulwarks: before action, heavy timbers or cables ('waist trees') were erected to protect the sail trimmers and fighting men. Top arming masked the crew from the aim of enemy musketeers and bowmen but provided no other safety. It consisted of two bolts of canvas, three feet six inches wide and painted in red, green, yellow and white, stretched round the waist in the form of a screen. Alternatively, parvesses or scantling were used; these were screens of planks of thin wood painted with shields like the Norse longships.

Ark Royal

Armada galleon

The sixty-gun *St Louis* was purchased from the Dutch in 1626 by Cardinal Richelieu, the 'Father of the French Navy'. She was one of the ponderous 'wooden-walls' which superseded the galleon. Cannon were improving and boarding parties became increasingly ineffectual; thus the waist had stout gratings to shield the crew from falling spars and debris, instead of nets to protect them from boarding parties. Rigging was now more complex, sails larger and more functional: they had buntlines and clewlines for furling like the later clippers. The bowsprit now carried a sprit topsail as well as the spritsail; fore and main masts carried topgallant sails and the mizzen – still lateen-rigged – a mizzen topsail.

The *Sovereign of the Seas*, launched in 1637, cost the then enormous sum of £66,000, raised by the Ship Money tax which helped to bring the downfall of Charles I. This ornately carved and gilded, three-masted, three-decked, 1,700-ton warship, with its impressive armament of 102 guns, was said to be 150 years in advance of her time. She was probably the first sailing vessel ever to carry royals above her fore and main topgallant sails and a mizzen topgallant above the mizzen topsail.

The Dutch-built *St Louis*

The *Sovereign of the Seas*, a 1,700-ton warship launched in 1637

She also boasted an elaborately-carved entry port very similar to that of HMS *Victory*, launched 128 years later. In 1652 *Sovereign of the Seas* was cut down to a two-decker by Peter Pett, son of Phineas, her builder, to increase her weatherliness, and thereafter renamed *Royal Sovereign* to commemorate the restoration of the monarchy.

Contemporary drawings of *Royal Sovereign* by Van de Velde the Elder show carving and gilding probably only equalled by the French, who protected it in battle with matting. The fighting efficiency of warships was beginning to give precedence to flamboyancy. In 1703 the Lords of the Admiralty ordered that ship decoration should be cheaper: by 1737 a mere £166.12.0. was allowed on the decoration of a first-rate ship and only £37 for a sixth-rater. This commonsense legislation had far-reaching effects, for soon the English man-o'-war became the standard vessel for many maritime powers.

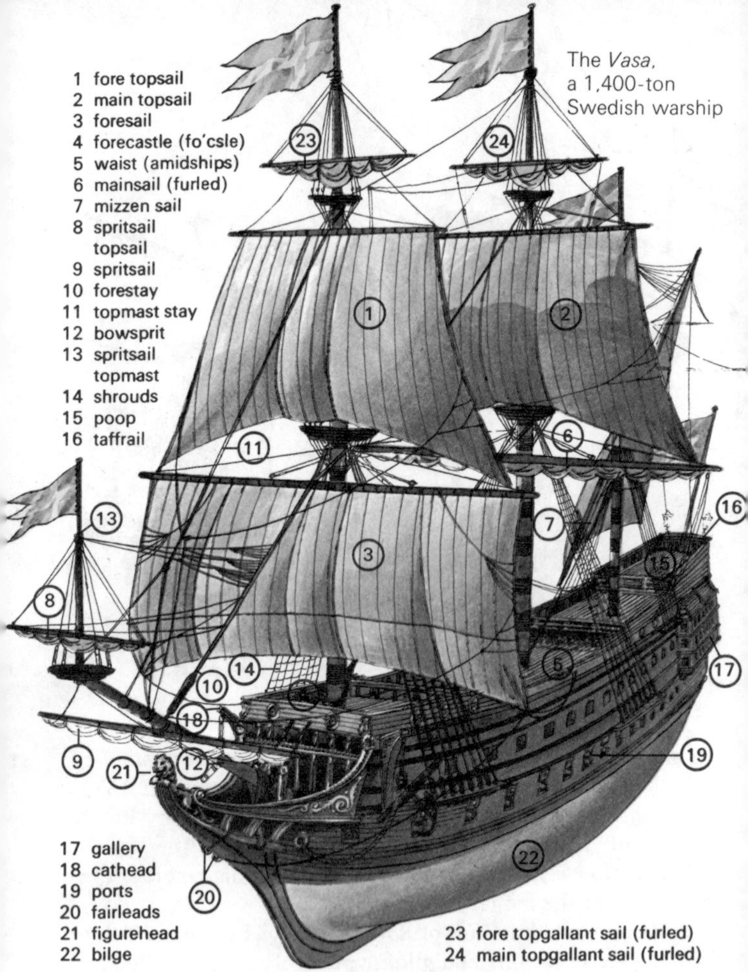

The *Vasa*, a 1,400-ton Swedish warship

1 fore topsail
2 main topsail
3 foresail
4 forecastle (fo'csle)
5 waist (amidships)
6 mainsail (furled)
7 mizzen sail
8 spritsail topsail
9 spritsail
10 forestay
11 topmast stay
12 bowsprit
13 spritsail topmast
14 shrouds
15 poop
16 taffrail

17 gallery
18 cathead
19 ports
20 fairleads
21 figurehead
22 bilge
23 fore topgallant sail (furled)
24 main topgallant sail (furled)

Typical of this type of warship was the 1,400-ton Swedish warship *Vasa*, launched before the Royal Palace of Gustavus Adolphus in Stockholm on 10 August 1628. Her only adornment was a huge, gilded and snarling lion figurehead, and ferocious-looking gilded lions' heads, set on a blood-red background, at each gunport. Before she had sailed a mile, *Vasa* was struck by a vicious squall, heeled rapidly on her beam-ends and, despite desperate efforts to trim the weight of the cannon, water roared through the open gunports and within minutes *Vasa* plummetted to the bottom. In 1956 she was located, and a complicated salvage operation began. On 4 May 1961, *Vasa* was towed triumphantly to dry-dock at Beckholmen, where her sodden timbers were treated with polyethylene glycol to preserve them. Finally *Vasa* was enclosed in glass and concrete as a unique maritime memorial – the world's oldest completely preserved and identified ship.

During the mid-seventeenth century, the Dutch were developing their own undecorated class of fighting ship: they had little time for adornment which could be obliterated with a single broadside. The two gun-decks of Dutch warships were well ventilated by spacious deck gratings, covered with tarpaulins in high seas. Dutch ships were generally swifter and handier than English or French vessels, but of lighter construction. So weatherly and efficient were they that Peter the Great, ruler of Russia, visited Holland as well as England to study shipbuilding for himself.

A 70-gun Dutch fighting ship of the mid-17th century

Ships-of-the-line

During the latter part of the eighteenth century smooth-bore cannon firing solid shot were reaching the peak of their destructive power. The formidably majestic ship-of-the-line was the most massively timbered sailing warship in history – counterpart of the great capital-ships to come.

Not the largest, yet most certainly the world's most formidable ship-of-the-line was the 102-gun HMS *Victory*, the flagship of Lord Nelson. Originally built at Chatham Dockyard between 1759–65 and twice rebuilt before the Battle of Trafalgar, *Victory* was made to withstand the shattering power of heavy cannon at close range, her double-layered hull, painted yellow and black, was of stubborn English oak, her 150-foot keel of iron-hard teak; her bottom was copper-sheathed against teredo worm. Such was the bulk of *Victory* that she needed 125 fathoms of nine-inch hempen cable to hold her safe at anchor.

With the exception of her stern carvings, covered quarter-galleries, entry port and figurehead, *Victory* was sparsely ornamented. On the lower gun-deck she carried thirty 32-pounders, each of three tons, known from their nine-foot barrels as 'long nines'. These guns had a range of one and a half miles, and each required a crew of fifteen. At 500 yards they could smash an iron ball through three feet of solid timber – the resulting splinter blast being lethal as a modern fragmentation bomb. The middle gun-deck carried twenty-eight 24-pounders, the upper-deck thirty 12-pounders, the half-deck ten 12-pounders and the forecastle head two 12-pounders and two 68-pound carronades, gaping monsters which fired 300 musket balls at close range and were called 'smashers'. The 102 guns consumed a formidable variety of shot, including grape shot (iron balls in canvas bags), fagot shot (iron cylinders which split into sections), dismantling shot (iron blades on a ring), chain shot (two cannonballs joined by a chain) and langridge (a form of shrapnel used to damage rigging).

Today, *Victory*, now in dry dock at Portsmouth, England, attracts 250,000 visitors a year.

HMS *Victory*, length 226ft, beam 52ft, 2,163 tons; above are the *Ohio* (*left*) and a contemporary French warship

A bomb ketch

A gun-launch

Unusual ships of war

The bomb ketch first appeared in 1682: a broad-beamed vessel converted by removing the foremast to clear space for the heavy mortars. The oaken 'knees' were changed for iron ones, and the deck was strengthened by heavy wooden 'beam bridges' against the shock of the trunnion-mounted mortars which lobbed a high-trajectory, 200-pound spherical bomb (the next most destructive missile known being a 48-pound solid shot). No recoil system of springs or cylinders yet existed: cannon were held by heavy ropes and tackles, to prevent them overturning on the gun crews when fired. Even the toughest sailors detested service in a bomb ketch, such was the terrible shock of the short-barrelled sea mortars' discharge.

Built by the Swedes for use against Russia from 1760–90, the shallow gun launch was the ancestor of the World War II gun boats. It was a lug-sail-rigged vessel which could also be propelled by oar, and armed with an 18- or 24-pounder cannon fired from the platform-like stern, built to save the crew running the gun in and out.

During the Napoleonic

The *chasse-marée*, a three-masted French lugger

Wars many British ships fell victim to the *chasse-marée*, a large, decked-in, three-masted lugger used by French privateers. These vessels were fast, armed with up to ten cannon ranging from swivel guns to 18-pounders, and manned by crews of between forty and seventy-five men.

Frigates

In 1793 the fast chebeks of the Bey of Algiers (see pages 20–1) took to attacking American merchant ships in the Mediterranean. In reply, the American Naval Act of 1794 instigated the building of six naval frigates to act as escorts to her merchant ships. One of these, the 2,200-ton *Constitution*, was launched on 21 October 1797. Her captain, William Baimbridge, had previously had the misfortune to run the US frigate *Philadelphia* aground off Tripoli, and been forced to surrender to the gun boats of the piratical Bey.

On 29 December 1812, cruising off Bahia, South America, was the British frigate HMS *Java*, under Captain Henry Lambert. She sighted *Constitution* and hoisted recognition signals; they were not answered and Captain Lambert showed his colours. The welterweight *Java* (forty-nine guns) and the light-heavyweight *Constitution* (fifty-nine guns) then joined battle. A musket-ball smashed into Baimbridge's leg, causing him to reel across the quarterdeck, and saving him from a cannonball which would have killed him outright. He continued to direct the battle propped against the bulwark.

Captain Lambert now tried to thrust *Java* against *Constitution*

The defeat in 1812 of the 49-gun British frigate *Java* (*left*) sunk by the heavier American vessel *Constitution*

in a desperate effort to board her but Baimbridge countered this manoeuvre by blasting *Java* away with furious broadsides. This was the turning point of the engagement. While the badly mauled *Java*'s crew – many of them veterans of Trafalgar – were still using short-range, inaccurate, smooth-bore muskets, the Americans were using rifles – probably for the first time in naval warfare.

Java fought on, until her last gun was silenced and she began to sink with her dead and wounded. The gallant British crew and their dying captain were taken aboard *Constitution*, where the sorely wounded Captain Baimbridge ordered his own bed to be brought up on deck for Captain Lambert. As the two captains lay side by side Baimbridge pressed the hilt of Captain Lambert's sword gently into its owner's numb fingers.

HMS *Java* had been sunk, sixty of her crew killed and 170 wounded. The American losses were only nine men killed and twenty-five wounded. *Constitution* remained on active service until 1881 and is now in the Boston Naval Shipyard, where, restored, and affectionately known as 'Old Ironsides', she recalls a mighty past.

The US corvette
General Pike

Corvettes and sloops

The corvette was one class smaller than the frigate, the sloop one smaller than the corvette. Both were light warships used for reconnaissance work, convoying, and as privateers. They were the first war vessels to adopt screw propulsion although they retained their sails and wooden hulls. One of the first vessels to incorporate the new with the old was the screw frigate HMS *Arrogant*, designed by J. Fincham of Portsmouth Dockyard, England, and launched there in 1848.

USS *General Pike*, launched in 1813, took only nine weeks to build. She carried twenty-six 24-pounder cannon and two short-barrelled 24-pounder carronades. So vastly out of proportion to the size of her hull was this corvette's spar and sail plan that it is interesting to compare some of her dimensions with those of the great clipper ship *Lightning*, (see pages 130–1) which was one of the most heavily sparred and canvassed vessels ever built.

General Pike: Length 174ft; beam 37ft; mainmast 195ft.
Lightning: Length 244ft; beam 44ft; mainmast 164ft.

Both vessels carried skysails on fore, main and mizzen masts. *General Pike* probably influenced the Baltimore clipper schooners (see pages 118–9) which sacrificed stability and all-round strength for speed.

The sloop has changed in appearance and function, but the first sloops were light warships, smaller than the corvette and frequently used most successfully for chasing smugglers.

The three-masted sloop shown is a model believed to be that of the 385-ton HMS *Cygnet*, captured from the French in 1779. She carried an armament of eighteen six-pounder cannon.

In later years the sloop underwent radical changes, becoming a single-masted, fore-and-aft-rigged vessel. There were two main types, the full sloop, with gaff-rigged topsail, mainsail and jib, and the Bermudan sloop with jib and a triangular 'leg-o'-mutton' mainsail.

The *Spray*, a famous vessel in which the lone sea-wanderer Captain Joshua Slocum sailed round the world between April 1895 and June 1898, was a sloop converted to a yawl. Built by Captain Slocum himself at the cost of only £111, this staunch little ship was under thirty-seven feet overall.

A three-masted sloop, probably HMS *Cygnet* (from a model)

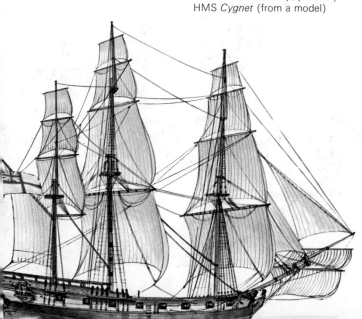

CARGO VESSELS

The East Indiamen

Built in 1717, *Geertruyd*, of 100 tons last (cargo-carrying capacity), 130 feet overall and manned by a crew of 180, belonged to the Dutch East India Company. On her third charter she made voyages to Batavia in 1718, 1723, 1727 and 1731.

Essex was famous as the greatest sail-carrier ever built, with a suit of sixty-three sails. On the mainmast alone she carried twenty-one sails, including three set above the skysail – the 'cloudscraper', 'moonraker' and 'stargazer'. She was probably the first camouflaged vessel, having one side painted differently from the other to confuse pirates.

Formed by Royal Charter in 1600, the British East India Company eventually became the most powerful organization of its kind ever to exist. By 1808 it had fifty-four ships, aggregating 45,342 tons, which sailed from London to India and China. A typical outward-bound cargo included household

The 130ft Dutch East Indiaman *Geertruyd*

The British East Indiaman *Essex*, with her suit of 63 sails

goods, watches and wines; a return cargo, spices, sugar, opium and ivory. In 1795, incidentally, the Company was able to lend the Admiralty fourteen of its fine ships and three thousand men.

Their captains were the elite of the maritime world, entitled to a thirteen-gun salute and a guard of honour on the arrival of their ships, and were also the wealthiest sailors of their day, making as much as £10,000 in a round voyage. Whilst their pay was only a token £10 per month, they received unheard-of privileges and perquisites – the most profitable of which was that of shipping out fifty tons of their own trade goods and bringing back twenty tons.

Whilst the East Indiaman was anchored off Deal awaiting the homeward-bound tide for London, the Revenue boarding officer would be splendidly wined and dined by the captain, whose contraband in the meantime was being loaded into the smuggling luggers of Deal! Then the luggers not infrequently made straight for the nearest enemy privateer, to sell the information that a fat prize lay in the offing.

The *Warren Hastings*, a British East Indiaman captured in 1805 by the French frigate *Piémontaise*

The richest prizes on the ocean, East Indiamen were, however, no easy prey: the biggest, of 1,200–1,500 tons, carried forty to fifty cannon, a highly competent chief gunner and well-trained gunner's mates.

On 14 February 1804, a homeward-bound fleet of fifteen East Indiamen led by Captain Nathaniel Dance aboard the flagship *Earl Camden*, were attacked by a French squadron in the Malacca Straits. The Squadron was a formidable one: the 1,200-crew ship *Marengo*, with seventy-four guns and three fine frigates, *Belle Poule* (forty-four guns), *Sémillante* (thirty-six) and *Berceau* (thirty-two).

With every stitch of canvas drawing, the East Indiamen *Earl Camden*, *Royal George* and *Ganges* bore down with such furiously sustained fire that the French squadron fled, pursued by the three victors for two hours.

The Frenchmen escaped in an action comparable, in modern terms, to the routing of a heavy cruiser and three destroyers by three armed merchantmen, at the cost of one death.

Equally gallant but less fortunate was the 1,200-ton East Indiaman *Warren Hastings*, with a crew of 196 and forty-four cannon. Homeward bound from China to Portsmouth, she was attacked by the French naval frigate *Piémontaise* on 21 June 1805. *Warren Hastings* was the bigger ship but had only about half the crew of the enemy frigate.

Warren Hastings fought mightily but the outcome was inevitable, for the French naval frigates of that period were the finest in the world – copied for their excellence by all the great maritime powers, including America. After a bitter battle of five hours *Warren Hastings*, with many of her crew dead and wounded and her foremast shot away, was towed off in triumph by the French. The sailing qualities and power of *Piémontaise* can be assessed from the fact that in only a moderate breeze and carrying only three single-reefed topsails, foresail and mizzen staysail, she towed her 1,200-ton, heavily laden prize at a constant seven and a half knots.

The last of the East Indiamen was probably *Elizabeth*, which left the Thames for China in the spring of 1833 and finished her voyage in Halifax on 18 August 1834 – the same year that the East India Company's charter ended, largely due to public disapproval of its monopolistic powers.

A Dutch whaleship

Whaleships

In 1650, when the British and Dutch were bitterly contesting the whaling grounds off Spitzbergen, the Americans first started whaling from Easthampton, Long Island.

Nantucket later surpassed Easthampton as a whaling port, to be surpassed in turn by New Bedford, which became the greatest and most colourful whaling port of all time – its ships leaving on voyages of up to seven years. For the lucky ones the rewards were great, for they brought back oil and whalebone from right and sperm whales valued at $100,000 and more. In 1862 the New Bedford whaleship *Corinthian* brought back a cargo worth $275,000. Others were less lucky, however, like the *Emmeline* of New Bedford, which after a voyage of twenty-six months returned with a beggarly ten barrels of oil.

These whaleships were square-rigged vessels, of 200–300 tons, flush-decked, broad in the beam and with deep holds to stow up to 2,400 barrels of oil. Their masts lacked the graceful rake of the clipper ships, and they could always be recognized from afar by the stains on sails and yards from the brick try-works, where the blubber was boiled down for oil. Space for cutting up the whales was essential, so the normally forward deck-house was moved aft and divided into two sections.

The whaleboats used for hunting the whale – unlike the

The *Charles W. Morgan*, an American whaleship

The whaleship *Ann Alexander*, rammed and sunk by a whale in 1851

lumpy parent vessel – were lithe and graceful boats of cedar planking, so light that two men could lift one and five oarsmen propel it at up to ten knots. The spare boats were kept on chocks between the main and mizzen masts, whilst five others were slung from derricks.

Their main equipment included a mast and spritsail, oars and paddles, harpoons so keen they could be used for shaving, lances for killing the whale and sharp whale-spades for cutting blubber. In addition there were casks of bread and water, two large tubs holding ropes for the harpoons, the main tub carrying 230 fathoms and the reserve tub seventy-five. These ropes were coiled with infinite care, for when the mad flurry of a harpooned 100-ton whale caused them to foul, the results were disastrous to both boat and crew.

Many of the whaleships' crews were raw countrymen who had never even seen the sea, and they often found their first encounter with the mighty sperm whale quite overwhelming.

Desertion and mutiny were more frequent in the whaleships than any other craft afloat. When hunted the sperm whale is not only ferocious but vindictive enough to smash the whaleboats, snap up their crews and even attack and sink the parent ship. This happened to the Nantucket whaleship *Essex*, rammed and sunk in the Pacific by a sperm whale on 20 November 1820 – an incident on which Herman Melville based his classic *Moby Dick*.

The lumbering, stinking whaleships of the early nineteenth century were true ocean pioneers, for they visited every bay, atoll and island of the Pacific Ocean and charted many new shoals and reefs. In the Galapagos Islands, then known as the Porter Islands, the crews of the far-roving whaleships established the Poste Restante of the Pacific Ocean in the form of a large turtle shell which served as a post box, where the crews of whaleships left and collected their mail – letters which had sometimes been written up to four years previously.

The *Eclipse*, an Aberdeen whaler

US naval brig of the 18th century

Brigs

The brig was square-rigged on both masts with a fore-and-aft-rigged brigsail on the mainmast (later known as the gaff mainsail). She also carried studding sails ('stuns'ls'), staysails, jib and foresail and, like fifteenth- and sixteenth-century ships, a spritsail on the bowsprit to steady the ship's head when running with the wind. There were large vents at each end of the foot of the sail to let sea-water run away quickly; perforated spinnakers of the twentieth century, which allow 'dead' air to escape may have evolved from these vents. Lofty-sparred and sometimes over-canvassed, the brig was a fast and handy vessel, usually armed with fourteen to sixteen cannon and employed both as despatch carrier and privateer.

The collier brig was a very different vessel. It appeared in the seventeenth century, when all coal was sea-borne from Newcastle and Sunderland to London. Large fleets of them plied the North Sea; in the month of September 1675 alone, a thousand collier brigs passed Thameswards through the Yarmouth Roads. A model of the 214-ton *Brotherly Love* is in the Science Museum, London. Built in 1704, she was still working in 1876. Seamen thought collier brigs were the lowest craft afloat. The crew lived in the worst imaginable conditions on the poorest food, luckily for not more than four days at a time.

The collier was loaded and unloaded by means of a big basket slung from the mainyard, hoisted by two or three men who gripped the whip and then jumped from a plank, their combined weight lifting the basket in and out of the hold. The innumerable shoals and sand banks of the North Sea are today littered with the wrecks of colliers.

The collier brig
Brotherly Love,
length 87ft, beam
24ft

Brigantines and snows

Early brigantines were identical in rig to brigs, except that the former did not carry a brigsail on the mainmast. During the first half of the nineteenth century the brigantine was a two-masted vessel which was square-rigged on the foremast and carried a fore-and-aft gaff mainsail and gaff topsail on the mainmast.

The American brigantine *Mary Celeste* – the most celebrated mystery ship of all time – was rigged in this manner. Built at Nova Scotia in 1861, of 282 tons and originally named *Amazon*, she seemed cursed from the start. Her first captain died on her maiden voyage, her second captain ended bankrupt and her third captain ran her on to the rocks. Her owners, fully convinced that she was cursed, sold her for a fraction of her value. Her next captain promptly ran her aground.

Again she was sold and her new owner, Captain J. H. Winchester of New York, rebuilt, refitted and renamed her, hoping perhaps, as sailors say, 'change her name – change her luck'. The name he chose was 'Mary Sellars', which a French painter wrote as *Mary Celeste*, and on 7 November 1872, loaded with 1,700 gallons of alcohol, she left New York for Genoa. Aboard were the captain's wife, baby daughter and crew of seven. On 5 December the *Dei Gratia* found her sailing erratically between the Azores and Portugal. When boarded,

The deserted American brigantine *Mary Celeste*

The snow, a brig-type coastal trader

her holds were found dry, her cargo unbroached, her occupants gone. The brig's boat, captain's chronometer and papers were also missing. A box of jewellery and a £5 note remained, and an unfinished letter from the mate to his wife. The last entry in the log was at 8 am on 25 November.

There were no signs of violence aboard but she had evidently been abandoned in a hurry. Her crew were never seen again. Feared and unlucky to the very last, she was finally wrecked off Cuba in 1885.

The snow was almost identical to the brig, but instead of a brigsail on the mainmast, she carried a snowsail on the snowmast or trysmast. This was an auxiliary spar stepped just abaft the mainmast and secured by an iron clamp to the afterside of the maintop. This prevented the squaresail on the mainmast from being fouled by the hoops of the snowsail as it was hoisted and lowered.

Cutters

In the early seventeenth century the Dutch sailed small, two-masted pleasure craft called jachts in their inland waters. Eventually the ship-wise Dutch decided that the jacht was too small for two masts and built a single-masted vessel from which evolved the cutter, a fore-and-aft-rigged vessel, which originally carried one and sometimes two square-rigged sails. So fast and handy were the cutters that they became the favourite vessel of Revenue forces and smugglers alike.

The two most notorious English smuggling cutters were *Swift* and *Ranger*. The latter was built at Cawsand Village near Plymouth, England. Armed with twenty-two cannon and manned by a crew of 100, she was so formidable during the 1780s, that she openly made regular landings of contraband near Torbay, Devon. The *Swift*, of 100 tons, with sixteen cannon and manned by some fifty men, also made regular landings near Torbay, bringing 2,000 casks of spirits and five tons of tea at a time. In her first year she paid for her building and running expenses and provided her owners with a handsome dividend.

These were but two of the many smuggling vessels which haunted the shores of southern England from 1750–1850. To combat them the hard-pressed Revenue forces had only forty-four cutters, manned by a total of 1,041 men. The largest of 210 tons and thirty men, was stationed at Colchester, Essex. The next largest were *Tartar* of Dover, Kent; *Speedwell* of Weymouth, Dorset, and *Rose* of Southampton, Hampshire, each of 190 tons, with twelve cannon and crews of thirty. It is probable that no two of these could have matched *Ranger* or *Swift*.

At this time the English smugglers were extremely powerful; the reason for their immunity lay in the connivance of influential people who enjoyed the huge profits and duty-free luxuries of smuggling.

Two young midshipmen of the Coast Blockade courageously engaged a big band of smugglers carrying kegs along Middle Street, Deal, in 1817. The midshipmen fought desperately, but were eventually forced to take refuge in a nearby shop by a huge mob of townsfolk. Mayor Edward Iggulsden promptly had the midshipmen arrested. At the trial Iggulsden, blatantly ignoring the evidence, gaoled them without bail on a capital charge of wounding a number of the smugglers. Luckily for the two young officers, Lord Justice Holroyd intervened and they were released to be rewarded with promotion.

A cutter, used alike by smugglers and Revenue men

The smuggling cutters finally vanished about 1860, discouraged by changing tariffs and a more enlightened public attitude.

Before the middle of the eighteenth century, the only way to reach the Channel Islands or the Continent from England was by chartering a private vessel. In 1781, however, the Government organized a fortnightly mail and passenger service between Southampton and the Channel Islands using smart cutters built almost exactly like the smuggling craft. One of these was the sleek and gracefully rigged *King George* which plied between Dover and Calais, from 1813–23, when sail gave way to steam. The first steam packets still carried sail on both masts. It is astonishing to reflect that in those early days mail packets sometimes turned to piracy when no mail was available.

Cutters were also popular with pilots, who had to reach deep-sea vessels as quickly as possible. The Bristol Channel pilot-cutter *Dyarchy* was one of these, built at Bristol in 1901. Other noteworthy cut-

(*Above*) the Government Channel cutter *King George*.
(*Below*) the Bristol pilot-cutter *Dyarchy*

ters were built for service in the North Sea; a number of them were designed by Colin Archer (who designed the *Fram* for Nansen, and *Ogre* for the pioneer yachtsman Ralph Stock). When cutters gave way to steam they were eagerly sought by yachtsmen who admired their seaworthiness and ease of handling.

One of the most famous – and smallest – cutters in the world was *Firecrest*, in which Alain Gerbault sailed from Cannes round the world between April 1923 and July 1929.

Almost frighteningly small for such long voyages, *Firecrest* was thirty-nine feet long with a beam of eight feet six inches. She was designed by Dixon Kemp and built by P. T. Harris, of Rowhedge, Essex, England, in 1892.

Solidly constructed of oak and teak *Firecrest* was divided into three compartments: a fo'csle with a cooking galley and two fresh-water tanks; a saloon with a folding table and lockers, and a two-berth sleeping cabin aft which also carried a fifteen-gallon fresh-water tank. This incredibly

Alain Gerbault's
Firecrest, length
39ft, beam
8ft 6in

staunch little cutter survived a blow of a kind which in the past had destroyed more than one fine clipper ship. Passing through the hurricane belt, she was overwhelmed by a toppling mass of broken water which thrust her clean beneath the surface, while her lone occupant, who had seen the breaker coming, took refuge up the mast.

Gerbault had the shattering experience of seeing his vessel literally vanish beneath him. She finally wallowed clear with only her bowsprit and part of her rigging gone.

Racing cutters

The intensely keen and costly rivalry between Britain and America for possession of the trophy now called the America's Cup stimulated the development and building of racing cutters as nothing else could have done, and the results were the most magnificent cutters the world will probably ever see.

Between 1851 – when Britain's challenger, the cutter *Laverock*, lost to the schooner *America* in the first race – and 1935, many famous racing cutters were built by both countries. Amongst these was Lord Dunraven's *Valkyrie II*, built at the then huge cost of £25,000, and memorable as the first of the big racing cutters to have a deep, fin-like keel, spoon bow and raking stern. Designed by Watson and very similar to King George V's beloved old racer *Britannia*, known as 'The Old Brit' by those who sailed her, *Valkyrie II* was beaten by America's mighty *Vigilant*, remembered for her revolutionary composite hull of lightweight steel and bronze and for her huge crew of seventy hands. The most famous Briton to be associated with the long line of so far unsuccessful British attempts to regain the America's Cup was Sir Thomas Lipton, who built the successive challengers *Shamrock I* to *Shamrock V* at a cost of something like two million pounds.

One of the stipulations of this historic contest was that the challenger had to sail across the Atlantic under her own canvas as did the first defender *America*. *Shamrock V* not only sailed across the Atlantic but, after losing the contest, sailed back again – straight into seventeen days of furious weather which ripped off her hatches, flooded and damaged her. A flush-deck racing cutter is not built for such conditions, and she was lucky to survive, limping at last into Southampton with her crew completely exhausted.

Sir Thomas would have built a sixth *Shamrock* but he died. In 1934 Mr T. O. M. Sopwith, an accomplished amateur yachtsman, built a new challenger, *Endeavour*, for £30,000. This splendid cutter, built on the American J Class design, had a displacement of 140 tons and a sail area of 7,500 square feet. The American defender *Rainbow*, also a J Class cutter, was designed by Starling Burgess, built at a cost of £80,000 and notable for her numerous labour-saving devices. The series of races between the two giants was the most keenly contested in the history of the America's Cup. It seems probable that *Endeavour* might well have returned to Britain in triumph but for the fact that Mr Sopwith, although a fine helmsman, was not in the same class as the professionals aboard *Rainbow*. In addition, a last-minute disagreement had deprived Mr Sopwith of some of his own professional crew.

Thus *Endeavour*, left in the hands of enthusiastic and competent amateurs, was beaten by *Rainbow*, sailed by equally enthusiastic and brilliant professionals. This was the last great race of the giants, for World War II intervened and the J Class cutters were laid up, never to race again for the America's Cup.

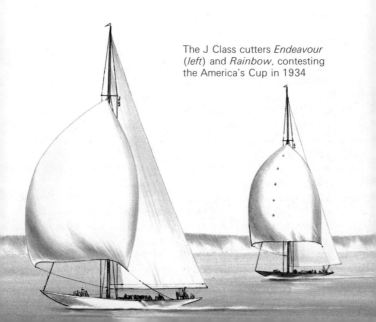

The J Class cutters *Endeavour* (*left*) and *Rainbow*, contesting the America's Cup in 1934

A North Sea ketch-rigged sailing trawler

FISHING VESSELS

The European ketch

From 1700–1900 the ketch was a common sight in European waters – especially the tan-sailed trawlers. Until about 1860 the main fishing ports of Britain were Brixham, Devon, and Barking, Essex. Pollution of the Thames led to the expansion of Great Yarmouth, Hull, and Grimsby, the home of the large trawlers of up to ninety tons. The smaller ones ranged from forty-five to eighty tons, the crews varying from four to eight men. The ketch-rigged sailing trawler was then the finest fore-and-aft-rigged vessel in Europe, its straight-stemmed, gracefully sheered and massively timbered hull being admirably designed to withstand heavy seas and the weight of the beam trawl as it dragged across the sea-bed. The crew lived in a cabin aft whilst forward was the boiler room for the steam capstan which hove up the trawl, two hatch-covered fish holds, an ice store, and the sail locker/storeroom in the bow. The powerful mizzenmast and mainmast raked slightly forward, the latter carrying a gaff-rigged mainsail, maintopsail, jib and foresail, whilst the mizzenmast – stepped well forward of the rudder head – carried a gaff-rigged mizzen and a mizzen topsail. When becalmed, trawlermen ingeniously spread a spare sail beneath the trawler's keel to catch the tide and thus keep the trawl moving.

In the first half of the nineteenth century, the North Sea was the world's richest fishing ground, and huge fleets of trawlers often remained fishing continuously on the Dogger Bank for three months at a time and more – a practice known as 'bulk fleeting'. Fast fish cutters raced the catches to the nearest port. Steam, the overfishing of the North Sea, and the opening of the Arctic fishing grounds, combined to put the sailing trawlers out of business.

Contemporary with the trawler was the cargo-ketch or billy-boy (see page 154). She was flat-bottomed, round-sterned, and fitted with leeboards. The ketches – probably due to their excellent construction – were notable for their longevity: the *Good Intent*, built at Plymouth in 1790, was still in service in 1928.

A trading ketch

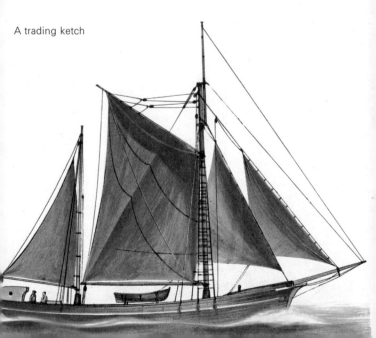

Yawls

The yawl, used for its excellent qualities by traders, fishermen and single-handed sailors, is not to be confused with the beach yawl (see pages 66–7) or the Skerries yawl (pages 154–5). The yawl proper is almost identical in rig to the ketch (pages 106–7) except that the ketch carries its mizzen sheet inboard and the yawl carries its mizzen sheet on a stern spar known as the bumpkin. Generally speaking the mizzenmast of the ketch is forward of the rudder head, whilst that of the yawl is stepped abaft the rudder head.

A famous yawl was *Islander*, built by Harry Pigeon, a farmer from the American Mid-West who did not even see the ocean until he was eighteen. He had an inherent love of boats and decided to build the yawl *Islander*. He gave her an iron keel weighing 1,250 pounds, a shallow hull, a coach-roofed cabin, extended above the deck, and a self-bailing cockpit, emptied

The yawl *Islander*, length 34ft, beam 10ft 9in, which sailed round the world in 1921–5

Gypsy, a yawl-rigged well smack

by means of pipes through the hull. She had hand-hewn planks and timbers of Douglas fir, Oregon pine and oak. Carrying a sail area of 633 square feet, *Islander* was built in eighteen months at a cost of £250. After acquiring some experience at sea Pigeon set out alone to sail around the world. He arrived back in Los Angeles on 31 October 1925 – to toss the old blue water shell-backs' direst insult, 'Farmer!' back in their teeth.

From 1860–1910, a fleet of fourteen yawl-rigged well smacks sailed from Aldeburgh, Suffolk, to the Iceland Banks, returning with up to two thousand live cod in their special 'wells'. Yacht-like in their graceful rig, they were the last of a proud tradition, for among their crews were direct descendants of the 'Fisherman Venturers' who, Aldeburgh's Elizabethan chronicles tell us, would 'yearly man fourteen ships to Iceland and the North to bring back thirty to forty thousand cod and ling to the great comfort and relief of the Queen's ministers and subjects'.

SCHOONERS, BARQUES, BARQUENTINES AND CLIPPERS

British and American schooners

Although it is said that the word 'schooner' was first used in Gloucester, Mass., in 1713, the Dutch were using schooner-rigged vessels as early as the seventeenth century. From these Dutch prototypes developed a type of sailing vessel used wherever speed and manœuvrability were essential – for carrying perishable cargoes, for fishing, war, slaving and racing.

Schooners fall into three main classes: topsail schooners, fore-and-aft-rigged with square-rigged topsails; hermaphrodite schooners, with fore-and-aft- and square-rigged sails on all masts; and fore-and-aft schooners which carried only fore-and-aft sails. These three basic types were also classified according to nationality and purpose: the Great Lakes schooners of America and Canada; the Atlantic Schooners, which included the Maine, Marblehead, Baltimore clipper, 'Gaspé'

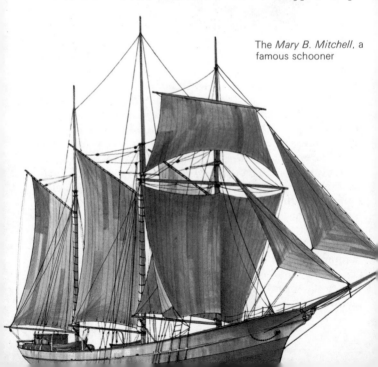

The *Mary B. Mitchell*, a famous schooner

A Marblehead schooner

and Grand Banks schooners. 'Plumb-stem' and 'file-bottom' schooners were so named because of their distinctive features.

Built at Carrickfergus, Co. Antrim, Ireland, in 1892, the 210-ton, three-masted schooner *Mary B. Mitchell* looked like a helpless old sea-spinster. While she lay in Falmouth Harbour loading china-clay during World War I the British Admiralty transformed her. Deck-housing which collapsed at the touch of a lever hid 12-pounder guns; she carried a radio transmitter and a gymnasium to keep her hand-picked crew fit for battle. Thereafter she sailed regularly from Falmouth, ostensibly as the dowdy old *Mary Y. José* of Vigo, but in reality a Naval 'Q' or 'Mystery' Ship, designed to destroy German submarines. On 2 December 1916 she sank the German submarine U26 and later, in the Mediterranean, she sank two more in one day, on 30 June 1917.

Possibly developed from the Chesapeake Bay schooner around 1750, the Marblehead schooner was a fast, two-masted, fore-and-aft-rigged vessel, from sixty to eighty feet overall, and up to ninety tons' displacement. She carried a crew of

The 75ft *Armistad*, a schooner which carried slaves from Cuba to the United States

some thirty or forty hands, and in time of war could be armed with eight to twelve 10-pounder cannon; normally she was used for trading and fishing.

The American privateer *Prince de Neufchâtel* was an hermaphrodite schooner, that is, she carried both square-rigged and fore-and-aft-rigged sails on both masts. Unlike the lumbering, bluff-bowed wooden warships of her time, this splendid schooner was fast and lean. In 1813 she snapped up nine British prizes in swift succession in the English Channel. Then, leaving prize crews on board, she put into Cherbourg laden with spoils. She captured six more prizes from 4–10 June and later, in the Irish Sea, she captured ten brigs, two sloops, a cutter and a British privateer. Frequently chased by British warships, her speed under an enormous press of sail was often more than twice that of her pursuers.

On Boxing Day 1814, however, disaster struck. *Prince de*

Neufchâtel, sighted in half a gale by three British frigates, started to flee and, indeed, was outstripping her enemies, when suddenly the tremendous stress of her vast sail area sprung her masts. Captured and taken to England, she seemed to prefer death to dishonour, for later she broke her back on the sill of the dock gate as she was leaving for service with the British Navy.

The *Armistad* though smaller than the *Neufchâtel*, was similar in appearance. She was a slaver, engaged in bringing negroes from Cuba to the United States. In 1839 a consignment of slaves, led by their chief, killed the captain and overpowered the crew, forcing one of them to turn and head the ship for Africa. Short of food, they decided first to put into Long Island to forage, and were promptly captured by a naval detachment. They were acquitted after a two-year trial which much inflamed the slavery question.

The American privateer *Prince de Neufchâtel*

Among the many tasks of the ubiquitous schooner was that of piloting larger vessels. The Sandy Hook pilot-schooner *Anna Maria*, built in 1819–20, was a typical example.

Because of their splendid sailing qualities and ease of handling schooners became the first pleasure craft, used exclusively for leisure purposes; later they were developed into racing yachts. The first and most famous of these was the *America*, built in answer to a challenge from British racing

The Sandy Hook pilot-schooner *Anna Maria*, length 58ft 11ins, beam 17ft 3ins, built 1819–20

The famous racing schooner *America*, launched in 1851, length 101ft 9ins, beam 23ft

yachtsmen and launched on 1 May 1851. With her slender black hull, low free-board, sharp bow, rounded stern and two masts which raked aft at an angle of five degrees, she could well have been a privateer. She had a displacement of 146 tons, and her suit of fore-and-aft-rigged cotton sails, (machine-woven to give lightness) totalled nearly 585 square yards.

After sailing across the Atlantic to England she beat the best British yachts in a controversial race. Her prize, a cup presented by the Royal Yacht Squadron, was valued at $500. Now called the America's Cup, it has remained in America, although Britain and Australia have spent at least $20,000,000 trying to regain it. Sold in England, *America* returned to her birthplace during the American Civil War. She served with the Confederate Navy as a blockade runner and after being scuttled to avoid capture in St John's River, Florida, was salvaged and served with the Union Navy until the end of the war.

As its name implies, the Baltimore clipper schooner originated from Baltimore. Designed for maximum speed, it was employed by the US Navy, privateers, smugglers and slave traders from about the middle of the eighteenth century.

The inherent weakness of the clipper schooner was that stability and seaworthiness were sacrificed for speed – which demanded a shallow-draught hull of low free-board, together with over-sparring and over-canvassing. Because of this many of the early clipper schooners were lost with all hands in squalls and rough weather.

Deeply concerned by these events, Captain J. W. Collins of Gloucester, Mass., and Mr J. D. Lawlor of New Brunswick, developed the 'plumb-stem' schooner, the most notable of their vessels being *Grampus*, launched in 1886. They were straight-stemmed, with a narrow, elliptical stern, narrower in beam but eighteen inches deeper in hull than the clipper schooners. This gave them a greater grip on the water and thus greater stability. They were generally regarded as one of the fastest, most seaworthy and successful types of schooners ever developed.

A further development of the plumb-stem schooner was the 'knockabout', which had a curved stem and no bowsprit. The first knockabout was built at Essex, Mass., in 1902, and named *Helen E. Thomas*; she was the forerunner of McManus's magnificent Grand Banks schooner *Elsie*, launched in 1910, which had a total sail area of 1,030 square yards.

The Grand Banks schooners were possibly the finest fore-and-aft-rigged schooners ever built, being magnificently weatherly, fast, easily handled and splendidly proportioned. Their crews fished from small flat-bottomed boats called dories, using miles of 'trawl' (lines, not nets). They also took part in the International Schooner Races from 1922–39.

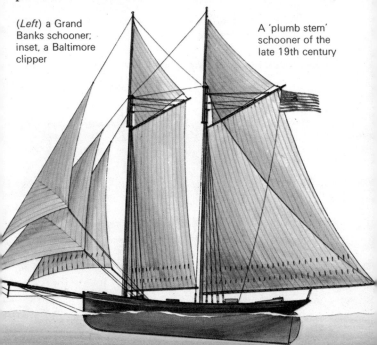

(*Left*) a Grand Banks schooner; inset, a Baltimore clipper

A 'plumb stem' schooner of the late 19th century

The Great Lakes cover 95,000 square miles, the world's largest expanse of fresh water, which in some aspects resembles the North Sea and Thames Approaches. Both have narrow, winding channels, dangerous shallows, variable winds, sudden and violent squalls and swiftly rising, steep and ugly seas, short of fetch but lethal of impact. Sailing vessels thus had to be specially designed, and to meet these conditions, *Griffin*, first of the Great Lakes vessels (1679), was a 60-ton craft modelled on a Dutch North Sea galliot.

As American and Canadian industry and agriculture expanded, bulk cargo carriers became necessary and so it was that Great Lakes schooners like the *E. W. Morrison* were developed. They were graceful but durable two- and three-masters, fore-and-aft-rigged and ranging between 100–777 tons. All of them had the special 'Great Lakes rig' to enable them to wear and tack quickly in rapidly shifting winds.

Maine was notable for its fine wooden four-masted schooners, and a typical example was the fore-and-aft-rigged *Helen Barnet Gring*. This clipper-bowed flush-decker was designed by J. J. Wardwell, of Rockland, and built by R. L. Bean at Camden.

The *Gring* was an offshore trader carrying both deck and hold cargoes, with a gross tonnage of 1,226, and an overall length of 203 feet. She was launched on 29 July 1919 in Japanese style: garlands of red roses were thrown and white

The *E. W. Morrison*, one of the Great Lakes schooners

The *Helen Barnet Gring*, a four-masted schooner built in Maine

pigeons released to mark the occasion. Her cargoes were, less romantically, phosphates and fertilizer (goat manure).

Sailing from Norfolk to Calais, Maine, loaded with coal, the *Gring* rammed the three-masted New London schooner *William Booth*, at 1 am on 26 April 1928, near the Vineyard Shoals, so violently that *William Booth* sank in five minutes. The crew of five were taken aboard the badly damaged *Gring*, which was forced to anchor and summon the coastguard for a tow into Boston.

At this period the cargo schooners were fighting a losing battle with steamships as bulk carriers and, after a short spell of carrying coal, the *Gring*, with many other schooners, was laid up at Boothbay, Maine, in 1932. Five years later she was recommissioned and, in 1940, loaded with goat manure, she tore out her bottom on Cayo Verde, Cuba, and became a total wreck. Her last moments were marked with untimely comedy, for the mate, bored with waiting, took to the rum bottle and turned his revolver on the captain's chickens.

Multi-masted vessels

Schooners of over 300 tons were considered unwieldy and the really big ones had the ugly nickname 'man killers' – an appellation which had some justification, for the ponderous main booms of the huge fore-and-aft sails often flailed the deck in rough weather or squalls and many an unfortunate seaman was crushed or knocked overboard.*

In spite of this, from the end of the nineteenth century to after the end of World War I, America built a number of large, multi-masted schooners in a last, forlorn attempt to compete with steamships as bulk cargo carriers. These schooners, with hulls like large clippers, barques or barquentines, were at best ungraceful, and at worst they were floating monstrosities.

The first of the five-masters was *Governor Ames*, of 1,778 tons gross, which, following in the wake of her betters, sailed

* During a race, the second mate of HM King George V's *Britannia* was knocked overboard and lost.

from New York via Cape Horn to San Francisco. The ferocious gales and cliff-like grey-beards of the Horn were successfully faced and ridden, although the menace of her massive booms must have been considerable.

The two largest of the five-masters were the *Nathaniel T. Palmer*, 2,440 tons gross, and the *John B. Prescott*, 2,454 tons gross, both of which were launched in 1898. A few six-masters, cheaply built, wooden 'utility' ships, appeared in 1900: these included the *George W. Wells*, 2,970 tons gross of Boston and the *Eleanor A. Percy*, 3,401 tons gross of Bath, Maine. The largest of the six-masters, and certainly the largest wooden ship, *Wyoming*, was built at Bath in 1909 to carry 5,000 tons of coal, manned only by a crew of twelve. This giant, 3,730-ton schooner was lost in March 1924, when after leaving Chesapeake Bay with a cargo of coal, she was wrecked on the American coast.

The steel schooner *Thomas W. Lawson* was the only seven-masted schooner every built and she emphasized the impracti-

(*Left*) the five-masted *John B. Prescott*

The 3,730-ton *Wyoming*, length 329ft, beam 50ft

cability of such huge, many-masted freaks. American seamen hated her for she was as ponderous in her movements as an old-time wooden ship-of-the-line, and even harder to handle.

Designed by Mr B. B. Crowninshield of Boston and built as a coal-carrier by the Fore River Shipbuilding Company of Quincy, Mass., she was launched in 1902. Her composite masts were 195 feet from truck to deck, the topmasts being of wood and the 135-foot lower masts of steel. When fully loaded she drew twenty-eight feet of water and when sailing light in water ballast she drew thirteen feet.

With a full cargo *Thomas W. Lawson* drew ten feet more than the specially constructed heavy-weight carrier *Beljeanne*, completed on the Tyne in 1926. The record load of this 10,170-ton, diesel-driven vessel was twenty-four railway coaches, twenty locomotives, two tugs and one motor tank barge.

The total sail area of the *Thomas W. Lawson* was approximately 4,444–5 square yards, just a little over one-third of the

The 5,218-ton schooner *Thomas W. Lawson*, length 404ft, beam 50ft

The *Werner Vinnen*, a five-masted steel schooner built in Germany

sail area of some of the earlier clippers which were a quarter her size. *Thomas W. Lawson* – a disappointment to all – had a short life, for she was lost in the entrance to the English Channel in 1908.

Prompted largely by economic necessity, Germany followed America in the building of large, multi-masted schooners, and in 1922 a fleet of five-masted steel schooners, equipped with auxiliary power in the form of surplus diesel engines taken from World War I submarines, was built for the firm of Vinnen, of Hamburg.

One of this fleet, *Werner Vinnen*, of 1,859 tons gross, plied the South American trade route until 1936. She was remarkable for her unique sail-plan of square-rigged sails on her fore- and mizzenmasts – a rig which classified her, more or less, as an hermaphrodite schooner.

Few vessels had such a varied and unusual career as the six-masted American barquentine *E. R. Sterling*. Originally built as the iron, four-masted *Lord Wolseley* by Harland and Wolff of

The *Nightingale*, a three-masted US schooner

Belfast in 1883, she was 308 feet overall, with a beam of forty-three feet. Dismasted off Cape Flattery in 1903, she was written off by the underwriters and acquired by C. E. Peabody of Vancouver who had her re-rigged as a six-masted barquentine – square-rigged on the mainmast but otherwise fore-and-aft-rigged. This made her slower, but easier to handle, and allowed her crew to be reduced from twenty-eight to seventeen.

In 1910 the barquentine was purchased by a well known American clipper-ship master, E.R. Sterling, who converted her into a modern floating home complete with motor launch and car. On Independence Day 1927, she lost her main- and mizzen-masts in a gale off the Falkland Islands. On 4 September the same year she was again dismasted, near the Cape Verde Islands and the first mate was crushed to death.

E.R. Sterling eventually limped into the Thames after a passage of 286 days out from Adelaide. Almost a floating wreck, she was sold for £4,000 to the Sunderland shipbreakers.

Considered to be the finest full-rigged ship ever built in America, the *Henry B. Hyde*, launched at Bath, Maine, in

November 1884, was of 2,583 tons, 268 feet long, with a beam of forty-five feet. Under Captain Phineas Pendleton III, a notorious driver of both ships and men, she was known as a 'damned Yankee hot-box'.

A hard, occasionally brutal man, Captain Pendleton was also a splendid seaman, for during her maiden voyage from New York to San Francisco in 1885 *Henry B. Hyde* lost her foremast and main topgallant mast in a heavy squall in the Doldrums. Undeterred, Captain Pendleton re-rigged her at sea, and reached San Francisco after 123 days. She loaded wheat and reached Liverpool ninety-six days later, returning to New York against head winds in the magnificent time of twenty-two days. This remarkable voyage firmly established the reputation of both ship and master among merchants. After eight voyages *Henry B. Hyde* was taken over by Captain Phineas Pendleton Jr, eventually to become a coal carrier.

Leaving New York on 11 February 1904, she was driven ashore during a full gale. After being refloated, she ran aground again, broke in two, and became a total wreck.

The 2,583-ton *Henry B. Hyde*, length 268ft, beam 45ft; inset is the 2,578-ton *E.R. Sterling*

The *Gatherer*, a three-masted barque, length 208ft, beam 40ft, built for the Pacific grain trade and ruled by a notably cruel captain, John Sparks, and his brutal mate, 'Black' Charley Watt

Like the barquentine, the barque – a vessel of three to five masts, square-rigged on all but the aftermast, which was fore-and-aft-rigged – needed fewer men to handle it and thus began to oust the full-rigged ship as a general cargo carrier.

The *Gatherer* was a three-masted, 1,509-ton barque built for the Pacific Coast grain trade – one of the 'Down Easters' built in the 'Down East' ports of Maine, Massachusetts, New Hampshire and Connecticut. Large, soft-wood ships with short lives, they had to make money quickly. Crews were regarded as expendable, and worked beyond endurance, brutally beaten and even killed. Their masters and mates became bywords for cruelty and sadism, and the ships became known as 'blood boats'.

Gatherer, under the demoniac sway of skipper John Sparks, became the infamous 'Bloody Gatherer', queen of the 'blood boats'. Off Cape Horn, a Scandinavian sailor scrambled aloft to the royal yard, cursed Sparks roundly and jumped to his death. Another sailor cut his throat and a third was shot by the mate, 'Black' Charley Watt.

The *James Baines* was a

luxuriously appointed vessel of 2,275 tons built about 1850 by Donald Mackay of Boston and named after her owner.

Her long, sharp, rakish bow was adorned with a figurehead of Mr Baines; her stern has been judged 'perfect' by the most exacting purists. Her masts and sparring were immensely heavy, for she carried 13,000 square yards of canvas in a single suit of sails. The crew lived in a spacious fo'c'sle, whilst abaft the foremast was a roomy deck-house leading to the luxurious passenger accommodation. She made her most famous passage under Captain MacDonald, leaving Britain on 9 December 1854 and arriving at Melbourne in the splendid time of sixty-three days. She carried 700 passengers, eighty of them First Class, and 1,400 tons of cargo and 350 sacks of mail, which under a penalty clause she had to deliver within sixty-five days.

The spectacular end of *James Baines* came on 22 April 1858. While she was discharging cargo at Liverpool, smoke was seen coming from her main hatch. The fire ran through the ship with devastating speed, and by nine o'clock that night the *James Baines* 'resembled a huge floating cinder'.

The 2,275-ton *James Baines*, length 260ft, beam 44ft 9ins

1 foremast	12 fore upper topsail	17 main lower topsail
2 mainmast	13 fore topgallant	18 main upper topsail
3 mizzenmast	14 fore royal	19 main topgallant
4 bowsprit	15 staysail	20 main royal
5 jibboom	16 mainsail	21 main skysail (furled)
6 martingale		22 mizzen crojack
7 flying jib		23 mizzen lower topsail
8 outer jib		24 mizzen upper topsail
9 inner jib		25 mizzen topgallant
10 fore course		26 mizzen royal
11 fore lower topsail		27 studding sails

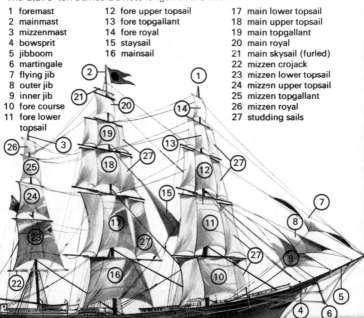

The famous American clipper *Lightning* was built as a passenger and emigrant ship in 1853–4 by the great Boston shipbuilder, Donald Mackay. Built like an axe to cleave the water, *Lightning* was a long, narrow ship with a finely moulded bow which blended classically into the sheerline and cutwater. The figurehead was a goddess bearing a golden thunderbolt in her outstretched hand. Even in an era of over-sparred ships, her masts and yards were awesome. Her mainmast was 164 feet from truck to deck, foremast 151 feet and mizzen-mast 115 feet. Her massive mainyard was ninety-five feet long and her lower studdingsail booms sixty-five feet. Her sail area was enormous: a total of 13,000 square yards of canvas included a moonraker crowning her mainmast, a distinction shared only by the *James Baines*.

She was splendidly appointed: the main saloon was eighty-six feet long, and her catering facilities would not have dis-

The *Lightning*, length 244ft, beam 44ft, 1,468 tons

Red Jacket, a rival clipper to *Lightning*, length 260ft, beam 44ft, 2,460 tons

graced a small modern passenger-cargo vessel.

Designed by the famous Boston ship designer Samuel A. Pook and built by George Thomas of Rockland, Maine, *Red Jacket* was named after the famous Red Indian Chief whose resplendent figurehead she bore. Intended as a rival to *Lightning* and launched just a few days before her, *Red Jacket* was the larger but her lines were less clean.

These two great ships made history in their transatlantic race of 1854. *Lightning* left Constitution Wharf, Boston, on 18 February and *Red Jacket*, commanded by the famous American packet captain Asa Eldridge, left New York the following day; both ships arrived at Liverpool on 4 March. During the race these two magnificent 'flyers' both reached speeds of eighteen knots, *Red Jacket* logging twenty-four-hour runs of 413, 374, 371, 343 and 300 nautical miles, while *Lightning* achieved 436, 328, 312 and 306 nautical miles. *Red Jacket* logged the total of 2,020 nautical miles in six days, a feat surpassed only by the incomparable *Cutty Sark*.

The famous tea clipper *Cutty Sark*, built in Scotland in 1869, length 212ft, beam 36ft, depth 21ft, 921 tons nett weight

The *Cutty Sark*, the greatest of all the clippers, was designed by Hercules Linton and built at Dumbarton, Scotland, for the tea trade in 1869. A mere 921 tons nett, 212 feet long with a beam of thirty-six feet, *Cutty Sark* carried a skysail on her lofty mainmast and divided topsails and upper and lower studdingsails on her foremast. Her slender lines and discreet decoration made her a thoroughbred indeed. As a tea clipper she was often beaten by *Thermopylae* – a clipper of such phenomenal sailing power she could 'ghost' at seven knots in airs so light that they would not extinguish a naked candle burning on her deck. However, *Cutty Sark* became supreme in establishing unbeaten records of sixty-seven, sixty-nine and seventy days from Sydney and Newcastle, Australia, to the English Channel. She now lies in dry dock at Greenwich, a memorial to the finest breed of ships the world has seen.

Built by Smith of St John's, New Brunswick, in the middle of the nineteenth century, the mighty 2,500-ton *Marco Polo* was the complete antithesis of the *Cutty Sark*. Noted for her massive pitch-pine timbering, she was built 'square as a brick fore and aft'. Purchased by James Baines and fitted out as a passenger ship, her accommodation was luxurious: the dining saloon, for instance, had a maple ceiling and pilasters panelled with mirrors and coins from every country of the world.

Most captains thought the *Marco Polo* too ponderous for record breaking. The notorious James Nicol 'Bully' Forbes saw, however, that the tremendous timbers and mighty masts of *Marco Polo* would allow her to be driven as few ships could be.

Forbes reached Australia from Liverpool in the record time of sixty-eight days, beating the steamer *Australia* by a clear week. 'Bully' Forbes drove her under full canvas through roaring gales, through the waves instead of over them, making the fantastic run of 1,344 nautical miles in four days. On one occasion frightened passengers crept from flooded cabins to beg 'Bully' Forbes to reduce canvas before he drove the ship clean under. Forbes laughed in their ashen faces and roared: 'We'll go to Hell or Melbourne!' Thereafter he padlocked the main sheets and stood over them with a revolver in each hand.

The *Marco Polo*, built 'square as a brick': int. length 185ft, beam 38ft, over 2,500 tons

Built at Northfleet on the Thames in 1853, the speedy 951-ton *Northfleet* saw notable service as a passenger and troopship, carrying troops to the Black Sea during the Crimean War and later between London and Hong Kong. In 1858, commanded by the excellent Benjamin Freeman, *Northfleet* caused a considerable stir in maritime circles by making the passage from Start Point, Devon, to Hong Kong in the remarkably short time of eighty-eight days seven hours. The same year, 300 miles from Lands End, she rescued nine men from the shattered Southampton brig *Hebe*, homeward bound from Alexandria.

On the ill-omened day of Friday 13 June 1862 the sea, as if in belated revenge for being baulked of its victims, wrought havoc with *Northfleet*. Outward bound from London to Hong Kong, she ran into squalls and giant seas, which pooped her twice – the most deadly assault any ship can survive.

Then, in January 1873, while waiting in the lee of Dungeness for a storm to subside, she was struck in the bow by a hit-and-run steamer. Despite all efforts, *Northfleet* sank in twenty minutes, carrying 293 emigrants with her. The ship responsible, the Spanish *Murillo*, was later identified by her damaged bow, although her name had been painted over. All British ships were compelled to show their name on the stern and both sides

The *Northfleet*, struck and sunk by a steamer off Dungeness in 1873

The *Tweed*, a converted steam frigate, length 285ft, beam 39ft 6ins

of the bows as a result of this tragedy.

The *Tweed* had a most unusual history. She was originally a steam paddle frigate named *Punjaub*, built for the Indian Marine and powered by two 700-hp engines. She was armed with ten 68-pounders, and saw notable service in the Crimean War, the Persian War and the Indian Mutiny.

The Indian Marine was absorbed by the British Royal Navy and *Punjaub* was subsequently purchased by the shipowner John Willis, who converted her into a full-rigged sailing ship. In 1863, she laid the Persian Gulf telegraph cable. Then refitted in Bombay as a passenger and troopship, she had all the virtues of a prime clipper after conversion and was fast in most conditions, under the driving leadership of her master, Captain Stuart. Finally, dismasted in a gale, she was towed into Port Elizabeth, and broken up.

A composite iron-
and-wood hull

COMPOSITE, IRON, AND STEEL SHIPS

Composite ships

The composite ship was invented by John Jordan, son of one
of the staff of J. H. MacIntyre and Sons, the Liverpool shipbuilders who launched the two first composite vessels ever
built. They were the schooner *Excelsior*, built in 1850, and the
barque *Marion MacIntyre*, built in 1851. It was a notable
advancement in shipbuilding, for the system combined the
strength of iron frames with the flexibility of wooden planking – and strength with flexibility is a prime safety factor in
ship construction. Its greatest fault was the galvanic action
produced by sea water between wood and metal. This was
overcome by fitting rubber insulation between the frames and
the planks, which were then secured by yellow-metal corro-
sion-proof screw bolts with countersunk heads. These were
stopped with a special composition after they had been
secured. The first composite tea clippers appeared in 1863.
They were the famous *Taiping* built by Robert Steel and Co.,
Eliza Shaw built by Alexander Stephen, and *Black Prince* and
Yang-tze, built by Alexander Hall. The smallest composite

barque ever built was the speedy and beautiful *Berean*, constructed by Pile of Sunderland and launched in August 1869. Her nett tonnage was 526, she was 160 feet long and had a beam of just over 30 feet.

She was unique in that her 43 ft-long quarterdeck was laid with knotless, butt-less four-inch-wide planks of New Zealand Kauri pine. Her deck-housing, topgallant bulwarks, fife rails, skylights, fo'c'sle panelling and ship's boats were all of polished teak.

Although small, she was notably sparred; her mainmast from deck to truck was 116 feet, foremast 112 feet and mizzen 93 feet. A dainty but not powerful ship, *Berean* could not be driven like the great clippers of her day and sailed her best in moderate weather with the wind two points abaft the beam. Her best day's run was 315 miles and she once sailed completely round the world in seventy-six days. At a period when accidents to both ships and crews were commonplace, *Berean*'s record was so accident-free that Lloyds of London offered to insure her at a specially reduced premium.

On one occasion she raced with the mighty *Thermopylae* to Tasmania. *Thermopylae* overtook *Berean* south of the Cape of Good Hope – storming along in boisterous winds under her mighty cloud of canvas. The great clipper was soon out of sight, but the race eventually finished with the little barque only seventeen hours behind.

The composite barque *Berean*, length 160ft, beam 30ft, 526 tons

Berean was commanded by Captain John Wyrill from the time of her launching until she was sold to the Norwegians in 1896. She spent fourteen years carrying ice from Norway to London, until in 1910 she collided with a steamer, and ended her days as a hulk off Falmouth.

The 663-ton *Coonatto*, the smallest composite full-rigged ship ever built, was 160 feet long with a beam of 28 feet. She was constructed by Bilbe of London in 1863 for the famous Orient Line. Her fine lines, together with Captain Begg's hard-driving capabilities, contributed further to her reputation as 'a wet ship'. She was fast: one splendid passage from Britain to Australia took only seventy days – this after broaching-to off St Paul's Island where huge seas swept both steering-wheel and helmsman overboard. She was finally stranded on the giant chalk boulders at the foot of Beachy Head, in 1872.

Built as a Blackwall passenger ship in 1866, *Sobraon* was the largest-ever composite ship, with teak planking on iron frames. She was 317 feet long, with a beam of 40 feet, and her sails totalled two acres of canvas. She had a registered tonnage of 2,131, and her hold was 27 feet deep. Yet in spite of this mountain of driving power *Sobraon*, unlike *Coonatto*, was a dry ship. In fact, she was so comfortable and luxurious that doctors frequently recommended her for health cruises. It was said that some of the cures achieved aboard this beneficent ship were little short of miraculous.

She was, however, no floating convalescent home: she could reel off a steady sixteen knots hour after hour and was probably the crack vessel of her time. During one voyage she

The *Coonatto*, length 160ft, beam 28ft

The 2,131-ton *Sobraon*, length 317ft, beam 40ft

covered 2,000 nautical miles in one week, whilst her best day's run was 340 nautical miles – both feats which few steamers of her time, or even later, could hope to equal. *Sobraon* was indeed a singular ship, for she carried her own animals for fresh meat, milk and eggs. She also carried several tons of ice and a fresh-water condenser – an almost unheard-of luxury in those days. And she was as seaworthy as well-found for in 1889, whilst northwards of the Crozets, she ran into hurricane-force squalls, which ripped her great sails to snapping 'Devil's bull-whips', and huge seas which swept away the entire length of the port bulwarks, together with a ship's boat and davits, and flooded the passenger accommodation.

When the wind dropped after three days, *Sobraon* rolled so violently in the huge swells while the damage was repaired that, but for the magnificent order of her standing rigging, her masts would have gone clean by the board.

After her last trip in 1891, she became an Australian Government reformatory ship for twenty years, and then was refitted as a training ship for boy seamen of the Royal Australian Navy.

Iron ships

The first iron ships were of 300–600 tons, but as the demand for greater cargo-carrying capacity grew, so did their size. Stronger and more durable than wood or composite ships, iron ships were more accident-prone. When overloaded, as ships frequently were, they rolled tremendously in rough weather and, being stiff, came back with a mighty jerk which threw a great strain on the ponderous iron masts and yards. Often the wire standing-rigging snapped and the ship was dismasted. Unlike wood or composite ships which had their standing-rigging set up from wide plates (chains) fitted outboard, the rigging of iron ships was set up from inboard, the span thus being too narrow to support the weight of masts and yards. These faults were eliminated by reducing the number of upper sails and yards, shortening masts and yards, and increasing the beam, thus providing greater span for the standing-rigging.

Patriarch was considered the finest iron ship of her time, with luxurious accommodation for forty passengers. The masts and rigging, designed by Walter Hood, were revolutionary: topmasts and lower masts were now in one piece, whilst the topgallant masts could be telescoped into the topmasts – a safe and easy method of reducing topweight in heavy weather.

The iron ship *Patriarch*, length 221ft, beam 38ft, depth 22ft, 1,405 tons

This innovation more than proved its worth, for although *Patriarch* carried heavy spars, including double topgallant yards at fore and mainmasts and a full suit of studdingsails, she was never dismasted in twenty-nine years' service between England and Australia. Her sea-keeping qualities were superb, and she was fast: on her maiden voyage, from London to Sydney, with forty passengers and 1,400 tons of general cargo aboard, she took seventy-four days, a record for an iron ship. Her best day's run was 377 nautical miles and her best week's run 2,060 nautical miles. She was finally wrecked south of the River Plate in 1911.

Tillie E. Starbuck, America's first iron full-rigged ship, had a deadweight capacity of 3,750 tons. She was 270 feet long with a beam of 42 feet. Her bowsprit and hollow masts were of steel reinforced with angle iron, and her suit of sails included three skysails bent to standing yards, a double topsail and a single topgallant sail.

Tillie E. Starbuck was something of a disappointment, being much slower than many of her wood-built contemporaries. She finally foundered off Cape Horn in 1907.

The *Tillie E. Starbuck*

Mermerus, with a registered tonnage of 1,671, was the most beautiful and successful of the clippers. She could carry 10,000 bales of wool worth £130,000, and delivered her cargoes as regularly as clockwork. She once reached Melbourne in sixty-six days. Ships tend to deteriorate with age, but not so *Mermerus*, for she maintained her fine performance to the end of her life – even after being sold to Russia in 1897. In 1904 she made a passage from Cardiff to Adelaide in seventy-three days and in the following year sailed from Adelaide to the Needles, Isle of Wight, in sixty-nine days.

Her end came on 29 November 1909, when, after leaving Frederickstadt with a cargo of timber for Melbourne, she ran aground in dense fog near Christiansand. After being refloated

Mermerus, a
1,671-ton wool
clipper

(*Right*) the *Slieve Roe*,
length 257ft, beam 38ft

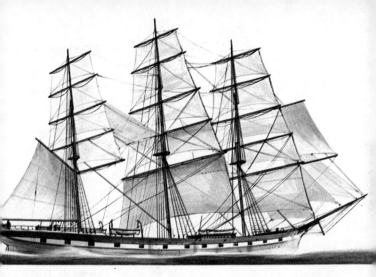

she was found to be too badly damaged for repair and was sold to the shipbreakers in April 1910.

Built by Harland and Wolff for the Indian jute trade and launched in 1877, *Slieve Roe* had a registered tonnage of 1,667 and a cargo capacity of approximately 3,900 tons. Her length overall was just over 257 feet. Unlike many clippers of her time *Slieve Roe* did not carry skysails and to offset this loss of sail area the size of her royals was enlarged. She also carried triangular sails called rafees, for use in fine weather. She represented the iron sailing ship at its best, for she was capable of sustaining a steady sixteen knots for up to twenty-four hours, her best day's run being 400 nautical miles.

She was also a happy ship, at a time when life aboard all clippers was hard and on some, sheer hell. Her first master wrote: 'It was a happy trip, for all the crew were young men. I think I was the oldest aboard, and I was only twenty-four. It used to be my greatest pleasure . . . to know that my watch were willing to jump once an order was given.'

Captain Ball, another master, said: 'I have listened to and read a good deal about famous ships and their captains 'Bully' this and 'Fire-eater' the other. It is a pleasure to think that those in charge of *Slieve Roe* could handle and drive a ship without turning a hair and without calling a man out of his name.'

Steel ships

Until about 1850 Germany's merchant fleet was small. But she
began to build vessels on British and American lines, until she
had some of the finest steel ships ever to exist.

Notable amongst these ships were those of the 'P' Line, ('P'
was their initial letter) which carried nitrates from Chile to
Hamburg. Most famous of all, and unique as the world's
biggest and only five-masted full-rigged ship, was *Preussen*.

Built in 1902, with a registered tonnage of 5,081, and a cargo
capacity of 8,000 tons, she was Gothic in her grandeur, with
steel masts three feet in diameter at their butts. Two powerful
steam engines housed on deck provided power to hoist and

haul, work the anchors, winches and steering gear and pump out water from the ballast tanks.

Built for the Californian grain trade in 1886, *Balclutha* (Gaelic *bal* = town; *clutha* = Clyde) had a gross tonnage of 1,689, and a cargo capacity of 2,660 tons. She was driven by a suit of twenty-five sails and manned by a crew of about twenty-six hands. For thirteen years she carried cargo all over the world and in 1899 she was sold to a San Francisco lumber company. She then served in the Alaskan salmon trade and, after being wrecked in 1904, she was sold to the Alaskan Packers' Association and renamed *Star of Alaska*. Finally she was restored in 1954 and is today preserved by the San Francisco Maritime Museum Association.

(*Left*) the *Preussen*, length 438ft, beam 54ft, 5,081 tons

(*Below*) the *Balclutha*, length 301ft, beam 38ft 6ins, 1,689 tons

Dirigo, known also as 'The Mighty Dirigo', was America's first all-steel sailing vessel – a four-masted barque of 2,845 tons register. Designed by J. F. Waddington of Liverpool, England, and built by A. Sewall of Bath, Maine, *Dirigo* had a cargo capacity of 4,500 tons, was steered by Waddington screw steering-gear from a steel helmsman's 'caboose' aft and carried the fantastic spread of 13,000 square yards of canvas, which included skysails and single topgallants. Yet in spite of her driving power the great barque's speed was unimpressive. Her greatest fault was that she was almost unmanageable when sailing in ballast: once, between Hong Kong and Honolulu she positively refused to go about when tacking, forcing her crew on eighty-one occasions to the laborious and sometimes risky expedient of wearing ship, i.e. changing from one tack to the other with the ship's stern to wind.

Leaving Seattle with a cargo of barley in October 1915, she was stopped by a British patrol boat off the coast of Scotland on suspicion of carrying contraband of war. Escorted into Lerwick, *Dirigo* was found to have a German crew member but was permitted to sail after her cargo was confiscated and the German

Dirigo, a 2,845-ton, four-masted barque, length 312ft, beam 45ft

The *France*, a huge five-masted steel barque – the largest sailing vessel ever built – length 418ft, 5,633 tons

interned. Jack London sailed on her from New York to San Francisco via Cape Horn to collect material for his novel *The Sea Wolf*. On 31 May 1917 she was sunk in the English Channel, torpedoed by a U-Boat near the famous Eddystone Lighthouse.

Before World War I France attempted to bolster her merchant fleet by building big sailing ships, frequently running them at a loss. One was the five-masted steel barque *France* – the largest sailing vessel ever built.

In 1919 she was chartered to take coal from the Tyne to America, leaving in December in the tow of a number of tugs, the largest of these being the French tug *Joffre*. All the tugs but *Joffre* left *France* almost as soon as she was at sea and a few days later barque and escort ran into a roaring gale which parted the towing warp. *France* vanished for several days and it was generally feared that she had foundered. Eventually, however, the battered vessel limped into the Firth of Forth and later continued across the Atlantic after repairs.

Finally she was lost at sea after leaving New Caledonia bound for Europe with a cargo of iron ore.

The *Esmeralda*,
length 285ft,
beam 42ft

MISCELLANY

Training ships

In an age of powered vessels it may seem odd that many
countries should employ sailing ships to train their seamen.
However, since a sailing ship is much more vulnerable to the
elements than a powered vessel she demands a great deal more
from her crew, including a far greater sense of responsibility,
urgency and awareness of danger. Clawing aloft on dizzily
reeling masts to fist-in vast areas of wet, wind-swollen,
thrashing canvas instils all this – and more.

Belonging to the Chilean Navy and launched in 1954,
Esmeralda is a four-masted schooner 285 feet in length, with a
beam of forty-two feet. Powered with a main auxiliary diesel
engine of 1,500 hp she carries over 3,000 square yards of sail.
This magnificent schooner was active from the day she was
launched and between 1954 and 1967 visited twenty-seven
countries. In July 1956 she also took part in the International
Training Ship Race from Torbay, Devon, to Lisbon.

The winner of the big class of sailing ships was an old
British ketch *Moyana*, built as a private yacht (before taxation
swept them from the seas), and manned by a crew of sixteen-

year-olds. *Christian Radich*, a full-rigged Norwegian ship, was second and *Ruyam* of Turkey third. The latter was a fine steel yacht originally built as the J Class racing cutter *Thistle* and re-rigged and re-fitted as a yawl in Germany. In the small-ship class the tiny, six-ton Italian yawl *Artica II* was first, the beautiful Argentinian racing yacht *Juana* second and the British naval yawl *Marabu* third.

Homeward-bound in the English Channel, *Moyana* ran into a full north-westerly gale and heavy cross-seas which damaged her rigging and opened her seams. The captain decided to safeguard her crew, and immediately radioed for help. It came swiftly in the form of the cargo-liner *Clan Maclean*, and within minutes *Moyana*'s entire crew was safe and the old ketch was left to die in harness.

Denmark's steel, three-masted, full-rigged ship *Danmark* was designed by Aage Larsen and built in the Nakskov ship-yard in 1933. Her gross tonnage is 790. Her mainmast is 130 feet above water level and she carries a total sail area of 1,955 square yards. She has an auxiliary 486-hp diesel engine.

Eighty boys aged fifteen to sixteen participate in six-month cruises, taking courses in all aspects of seamanship to prepare them as officers of the Danish Merchant Navy. Shipowners and the Danish Government subsidize this excellent scheme.

The 790-ton *Danmark*, built in 1933, length 196ft, beam 33ft

Lifeboats

Britain's Royal National Lifeboat Institution was founded in 1824 by Sir William Hillary and since that time its lifeboats have saved more lives from the sea than any other organization in existence. Before the advent of the magnificent modern power-driven, radio-equipped lifeboats, the work of RNLI was done by means of 'pulling-sailing' lifeboats, equipped with both oars and sails. These boats, though primitive by modern standards, were still highly specialized craft: they had to be small enough to handle but strong enough to endure the elements at their worst; to be able to free themselves continuously of a crippling weight of water, and be so buoyant as to remain afloat when swamped to the gunwales.

Although they were the most seaworthy and durable boats of their time the sailing lifeboats were much more vulnerable than the modern lifeboats, depending as they did entirely on sail and the strength of their volunteer crews.

One celebrated rescue-operation concerned the *Indian*

The Padstow Lifeboat

1 foremast	6 truck
2 forelugsail	7 shrouds
3 mizzen mast	8 reef points
4 mizzen lugsail	9 staysail
5 gaff	10 halyard
	11 sheet
	12 helm, tiller
	13 rudder
	14 stern
	15 keel
	16 stem
	17 bilge keel
	18 fender
	19 bulwarks

Chief, wrecked on the dreaded Longsand in the Thames Estuary on 5 January 1881. Bound for Yokohama commanded by Captain Fraser, she ran aground in a bitter easterly gale, with blinding snow squalls and vicious surf, which burst the hull. The crew lashed themselves to the tottering masts where many soon died of exposure. The captain was crushed by a falling spar and instantly killed. So great was the horror of this disaster that the second mate and nephew to the captain, Howard Primrose Fraser, lost his reason and died after being taken aboard the lifeboat. Four sailing lifeboats were launched, one each from Aldeburgh, Clacton, Harwich and Ramsgate. The brutal seas and wind defeated all the lifeboats except the *Bradford* of Ramsgate, under Coxswain Charles Fish, which was towed to the wreck by the paddle tug *Aid*. One of those rescued said later that he had felt safer on the wreck, as the lifeboat had seemed likely to be overwhelmed by every wave.

One of the larger type of fembøring, a single-masted Norwegian fishing vessel, length 44–50ft, beam 9½–12ft

Unusual coastal craft (1850–1950)

All ships, vessels and craft develop according to their function and environment. At one time, for example, Norwegian fishermen, restricted to fishing in one area, used a small, thirty-foot fembøring, which carried only one sail. Then, in 1857, the Lofoten fishery regulations were amended, and fembørings were enlarged to between forty-four and fifty feet in length, the single mast having a lug-type mainsail and a square topsail. The sails were either of canvas or homespun russet, and the vessel itself was built of pine or spruce.

In 1963 two twenty-six-year-old Norwegians, Jans Henrick Stemland and Odd Sorensen, set out in the 100-year-old fembøring *Victoria*, which they had bought for £10, to sail to Israel along the old Viking route. Unfortunately she began to leak, and after 2,000 miles they had to put in to London, where *Victoria* was shipped back to Stavanger to grace a museum.

Up to the end of the 1870s
two types of lugsail-rigged
craft, the skaffie and the fifie,
were used, mostly for fishing,
on the east coast of Scotland.
The skaffie, with its short keel,
was easy to handle when
going about, did not ship so
much water and had more
deck space than the fifie
which, with its longer keel
and deeper bow, behaved
better in a following sea.

The zulu, first produced in
1878, combined the best
points of both. She carried
high-peaked lugsails on mainmast and mizzen, and a long
bumpkin, or spar, to take the
mizzen sheets as in a yawl.
The mainmast could be lowered aft along the deck to
provide space for the hauling
of herring drift-nets. The zulu
was the fastest fishing vessel
in the British Isles.

The Manx nickie was a
carvel-built fishing craft,
with hardly any sheer, drawing more water aft than forward and unusual in that it
carried a mizzen staysail. Like
Cornish luggers, the nickie
had a sharp stern in preference
to a square transom stern, for
ease of manoeuvre.

The billyboy was a sea-going development of the Humber keel, the hull being larger, with stout bulwarks to give greater freeboard. Originally she carried the conventional Humber keel sail-plan (see page 68). Later, she was ketch-rigged for better speed and manoeuvrability. This coastal cargo carrier was a 'family ship', frequently operated by a skipper-owner and crewed by his wife and family.

The Skerries or Greencastle yawl was not yawl-rigged; the name comes from the Scandinavian 'jol', which applied to all double-ended boats. The Skerries yawl actually originated from Trondheim, Norway, and was thus also called a 'Drontheim' – presumably an Irish corruption of Trondheim. This unusual craft had a uniquely flexible rig, having a hole in each of the three forward thwarts, which permitted its two masts to be stepped in different positions. One method was to step one mast in the bow thwart and the second in the third thwart and then set the sprit foresail, gaff mainsail and a small jib. Or a single mast could fit in the second thwart and carry a

A ketch-rigged billyboy; this coastal cargo vessel was originally developed from the Humber keel

A Skerries yawl   A Shetland sixern

large standing lugsail and a large jib. The former alternative made the Skerries yawl the only schooner-rigged fishing craft in the British Isles.

Do-it-yourself boat-building kits are no recent innovation, for the Shetland sixern – so called because it could be rowed with six oars ('slates') when necessary – was shipped from Norway to the Shetlands in kits ready for assembly over a century ago, as suitable timber is scarce in the Shetlands.

The sixern had Norse lines, and was up to thirty-six feet long. The large dipping lugsail entailed dipping the yard round the mast each time the boat changed tack. The helmsman controlled the mainsheet and sat with his boot on the garboard strake, the plank next to the keel. When the sixern was driving dangerously fast the strake vibrated strongly under his foot. The sail would be lowered instantly and hoisted only when the vibrations ceased.

BOOKS TO READ

Alde Estuary by G. Arnott. Adlard & Co., Ipswich, 1952.

Boats and Boatmen by T. C. Lethbridge. Thames & Hudson, London, 1952.

The Clipper Ship Era by A. H. Clark. Putnam's Sons, New York, c. 1940.

The Colonial Clippers by Basil Lubbock. Brown, Son & Ferguson, Glasgow, 1924.

Forgotten Ports of England by G. Goldsmith-Carter. Evans, London, 1951.

The Last of the Wind Ships by Alan J. Villiers. Routledge & Kegan Paul, London, 1934.

Last Stronghold of Sail by Hervey Benham. Harrap, London, 1952.

Marshland Adventure by Wentworth Day. Harrap, London, 1950

The Romance of the Clipper Ships by Basil Lubbock. Harrap, London, 1958.

Sailors Sailors Sailors by G. Goldsmith-Carter. Paul Hamlyn, London, 1966.

The Shape of Ships by William McDowell. Hutchinson, London, 1956.

The Ship by Bjorn Landstrom. Allen & Unwin, London, 1961.

Ships Ships Ships ed. by Robina Farbrother. Paul Hamlyn, London, 1963.

Ships and Men by W. J. Bassett-Lowke. Harrap, London, 1952.

Tall Ships and Great Captains by A. B. C. Whipple. Gollancz, London, 1961.

ACKNOWLEDGMENTS

British Museum, London; Chilean Embassy, London; Corporation of the City of Aberdeen, Scotland; Italian Embassy, London; Marine Research Society of Bath, Maine; Mariners Museum, Newport News, Virginia; Massachusetts Historical Society, Boston; Missions to Seamen, London; National Bank of New Zealand, London; National Maritime Museum, Greenwich, London; Nederlandsch Historisch Scheerpvaart Museum, Amsterdam; Old Dartmouth Historical Society Whaling Museum, New Bedford, Massachusetts; Rijksmuseum, Amsterdam; Royal National Life-Boat Institution, London; San Francisco Maritime Museum; Science Museum, London; Smithsonian Institution, Washington, D.C.; Statens Sjöhistoriska Museum, Stockholm; Trinity House, North Channel Pilots Committee, Harwich, Essex; 'Yachting Monthly'.

INDEX

159

SOME OTHER TITLES IN THIS SERIES

 Arts

Domestic Animals and Pets

Domestic Science

Gardening

General Information

History and Mythology

Natural History

Popular Science

Arts
Antique Furniture/Architecture/Clocks and Watches/Glass for
Collectors/Jewellery/Musical Instruments/Porcelain/Victoriana

Domestic Animals and Pets
Budgerigars/Cats/Dog Care/Dogs/Horses and Ponies/Pet Birds/Pets
for Children/Tropical Freshwater Aquaria/Tropical Marine Aquaria

Domestic Science
Flower Arranging

Gardening
Chrysanthemums/Garden Flowers/Garden Shrubs/House Plants/
Plants for Small Gardens/Roses

General Information
Aircraft/Arms and Armour/Coins and Medals/Flags/Guns/Military
Uniforms/National Costumes of the world/Rockets and Missiles/
Sailing/Sailing Ships and Sailing Craft/Sea Fishing/Trains/Veteran
and Vintage Cars/Warships

History and Mythology
Age of Shakespeare/Archaeology/Discovery of: Africa/The American
West/Australia/Japan/North America/South America/Myths and
Legends of: Africa/Ancient Egypt/Ancient Greece/Ancient Rome/
India/The South Seas/Witchcraft and Black Magic

Natural History
The Animal Kingdom/Animals of Australia and New Zealand/
Animals of Southern Asia/Bird Behaviour/Birds of Prey/Butterflies/
Evolution of Life/Fishes of the world/Fossil Man/A Guide to the
Seashore/ Life in the Sea/Mammals of the world/Monkeys and
Apes/Natural History Collecting/The Plant Kingdom/Prehistoric
Animals/Seabirds/Seashells/Snakes of the world/Trees of the
World/Tropical Birds/Wild Cats

Popular Science
Astronomy/Atomic Energy/Chemistry/Computers at Work/The
Earth/Electricity/Electronics/Exploring the Planets/The Human
Body/Mathematics/Microscopes and Microscopic Life/Undersea
Exploration/The Weather Guide